FROM GOOD NEWS TO GOSPELS

From Good News to Gospels

*What Did the First Christians
Say about Jesus?*

David Wenham

WILLIAM B. EERDMANS PUBLISHING COMPANY
GRAND RAPIDS, MICHIGAN

Wm. B. Eerdmans Publishing Co.
2140 Oak Industrial Drive NE, Grand Rapids, Michigan 49505
www.eerdmans.com

27 26 25 24 23 22 21 20 19 18   1 2 3 4 5 6 7 8 9 10

ISBN 978-0-8028-7368-2

Library of Congress Cataloging-in-Publication Data

Names: Wenham, David, author.
Title: From good news to Gospels : what did the first Christians
    say about Jesus? / David Wenham.
Description: Grand Rapids : Eerdmans Publishing Co., 2018. |
    Includes bibliographical references and index.
Identifiers: LCCN 2017031076 | ISBN 9780802873682 (pbk. : alk. paper)
Subjects: LCSH: Jesus Christ—History of doctrines—Early church, ca. 30–600.
Classification: LCC BT198 .W4543 2018 | DDC 232.09/015—dc23
    LC record available at https://lccn.loc.gov/2017031076

Contents

Foreword by Donald A. Hagner   vii

Preface   xviii

Abbreviations   xx

1. Good News to Gospels   1

2. The Teaching of Jesus and
   the Story of Acts   13

3. The Evidence of Mark,
   Matthew, and John   27

4. The Evidence of Paul   36

5. The Oral Tradition in the Gospels   65

6. Two Examples of the Oral Tradition   74

CONTENTS

7. The Extent of the Oral Tradition 87

8. The Message of the First Christians 95

   Bibliography 109

   Author Index 119

   Subject Index 121

   Biblical References Index 122

Foreword

The earliest Christian writings were letters written to churches. These writings began to appear nearly twenty years after the death and resurrection of Jesus. It may have been as long as another twenty years before written accounts, gospels, began to appear. Thus, there could well have been a forty-year gap between the ministry of Jesus and the earliest extant records.

Of course, there may have been other Christian writings that are now lost. The forty-year gap was a period when the accounts of what Jesus said and did were transmitted by means of oral tradition. Scholars know very little about the exact content of the oral tradition, to which we lack direct access. It may well have varied in extent and exact wording from region to region. There is every reason to believe that early Christian literature preserves the oral tradition of those early decades.

The question immediately arises concerning the reliability of the early oral tradition. To modern ears, four decades of oral transmission sounds like the ideal way to guarantee the *unreliability* of the tradition.

A few decades ago some scholars came together as the Jesus Seminar, a group with a focus on identifying the actual words and deeds of Jesus. Their conclusions confirm the popular belief that "transmitters of oral tradition do not ordinarily remember the exact wording of the saying or parable they are attempting to quote."[1] The Seminar proceeds to give a "scientific" explanation: "Recent experiments with memory have led psychologists and others to conclude that the human memory consists of short-term and long-term memory. Short-term memory can retain only about seven items at a time. . . . One experiment has shown that most people forget the exact wording of a particular statement after only sixteen syllables intervene between the original statement and the request to recall that wording."[2] The members of the Jesus Seminar are apparently oblivious to cultural realities of the first century to which, for example, Birger Gerhardsson, among others, has called attention. They blithely assume that modern studies of memory are applicable without modification to the first century. They furthermore confidently assert that the evangelists "supplied dialogue for him [Jesus] on many narrative occasions for which their memories could not recall an appropriate aphorism or parable. In a word, they creatively invented speech for Jesus."[3] However, this

1. Robert W. Funk and Roy W. Hoover, eds., *The Five Gospels* (San Francisco: HarperSanFrancisco, 1997), 1.
2. Funk and Hoover, *The Five Gospels*, 28.
3. Funk and Hoover, *The Five Gospels*, 28.

opinion can hardly be more than pure speculation. In fact, it contradicts what is known about the first-century cultural setting. In short, in contrast to any "controlled" oral tradition, the Seminar views the oral tradition as "uncontrolled."

As David Wenham notes in the present book, recent decades have shown a resurgence of interest in oral tradition in the early church. James D. G. Dunn calls for moving away from the default setting where exclusive attention has been devoted to written sources of the gospels. His work has recently focused on the oral tradition underlying the gospels.[4] Many scholars debate the most appropriate cultural model for describing the process of oral transmission behind the written gospels. Werner H. Kelber argues from a socio-anthropological viewpoint for the repeated, variable oral performances of folklore in ancient cultures.[5] Kenneth E. Bailey, who worked for many years as a missionary in the Middle East,[6] proposes an alternative model. There among villagers he observed the oral transmission of various kinds of material with shifting degrees of flexibility (depending on the importance of the material to the identity of the community), handed on under the control of the community. Bailey character-

4. See James D. G. Dunn, *Jesus Remembered*, vol. 1 of *Christianity in the Making* (Grand Rapids: Eerdmans, 2003), 173–254.

5. Werner H. Kelber, *The Oral and the Written Gospel* (Philadelphia: Fortress, 1983).

6. See Kenneth E. Bailey, "Informal Controlled Oral Tradition and the Synoptic Gospels," *Asia Journal of Theology* 5 (1991): 34–54; and Kenneth E. Bailey, "Middle Eastern Oral Tradition and the Synoptic Gospels," *ExpT* 106 (1995): 363–67.

izes such tradition as "informal and controlled"—"informal" because there is no particular teacher or students in view. Anyone in the community can speak or "perform" the material in a particular setting. Remarkably, both N. T. Wright and Dunn opt for Bailey's model of oral transmission.[7]

Despite the use of Bailey's model, an important question persists: where can we find the most satisfactory explanation of the transmission of oral material *in first-century Jewish Palestine*? Would it not be most natural to look at the transmission of rabbinic material by memorization (a controlled and formal tradition) in Israel at the time of Jesus, as Gerhardsson has done?[8] Why go further afield to other countries, other cultures, or to the folklorists and the general phenomena of oral transmission? We may, of course, find some help here to understand the process of oral tradition behind Matthew, Mark, Luke, and John. However, doing so would mislead us as much as help us. It seems safer to stay close to the time and context of the gospels.

To be sure, Bailey's work is valuable in many respects. Yet, is it clear that the practice of telling community stories in Arab villages in twentieth-century Lebanon, Syria, or Iraq is a safe guide to what was going on in first-century Jewish Palestine? Where in the New Testament

7. Dunn, *Jesus Remembered*, 205–9; N. T. Wright, *Jesus and the Victory of God*, vol. 2 of *Christian Origins and the Question of God* (Minneapolis: Fortress, 1996), 133–37.

8. Gerhardsson's initial work, in the 1960s, was meant as a counter to Rudolf Bultmann's support for an informal and uncontrolled process of oral transmission.

or elsewhere in contemporary literature can one find any examples of, or references to, the community's communication of stories, the basis of Bailey's view?

The choice of this model of oral tradition over Gerhardsson's model is to my mind a mistake, and methodologically unjustified. It is related to two further oversights, to which we now turn.

A look at typical rabbinic practice in first-century Jewish contexts—such as Gerhardsson provides[9]—offers a stark contrast to the feeble memories of typical Americans. The Jesus Seminar neglects the uniqueness of the material in the gospels. I mean the uniqueness not merely of the *content* of the transmitted material but the dramatic importance of the whole *context* in which that material was given—i.e., the announcement of the dawning of the kingdom of God in and through the person of Jesus the Messiah now present among his people. These points deserve more attention than they are usually given.

First, the utter uniqueness of Jesus is of great significance for understanding the importance of the oral tradition from the beginning. Why is it that the disciples listened so carefully to his words, treasured them, and memorized them? It was because they had never heard authority like this before (e.g., Mark 1:22, 27; Matt 7:29; Luke 4:32) and because they had come to the conclusion

---

9. See Birger Gerhardsson, *Memory and Manuscript: Oral Tradition and Written Transmission in Rabbinic Judaism and Early Christianity* with *Tradition and Transmission in Early Christianity* (Grand Rapids: Eerdmans, 1998), and Birger Gerhardsson, *The Reliability of the Gospel Tradition* (Peabody, MA: Hendrickson, 2001).

that Jesus was the Messiah (Mark 8:27–30 and parallels). They were experiencing the most exciting time imaginable as they participated in the announcement of the good news of the kingdom, indeed saw it dawning in the words and deeds of their master. This was no ordinary teacher—let alone performing bard or storyteller—but a unique teacher with unparalleled authority. His authority was in a different category than that of the scribes, the scholars of the day. While they compared opinions, he spoke with an astonishing "*I* say to you."

Matthew, Mark, Luke, and John stress that Jesus was a "teacher" (he is very often referred to as *didaskalos*).[10] We frequently read of Jesus "teaching." Jesus as unique teacher is the point expressed in Matt 23:8, 10: "But you are not to be called rabbi, for you have one teacher (*didaskalos*), and you are all students. . . . Nor are you to be called instructors, for you have one instructor (*kathēgētēs*), the Messiah."[11] On the receiving end of the teaching are the "disciples" (*mathētai*), the specific learners who are taught.

When you have this kind of teacher, the very embodiment of authority, in this kind of situation, the analogy of rabbi and disciples becomes exceptionally appropriate. Does it not suggest that Gerhardsson is correct in look-

---

10. The use of the phrase "canonical gospels"—here and in the text of Wenham below—risks anachronism. It refers to the four texts (Matthew, Mark, Luke, and John) that would become canonical. The canonical gospels are distinguished in this argument (and in the argument of Wenham) from other gospels in early Christian literature.

11. See Samuel Byrskog, *Jesus the Only Teacher: Didactic Authority and Transmission in Ancient Israel, Ancient Judaism and the Matthean Community*, Coniectanea Biblica New Testament Series 24 (Stockholm: Almqvist & Wiksell International, 1994).

ing here for the model that underlies the later texts? If Gerhardsson is correct, it rules out an uncontrolled and informal process of transmission. "Informal" tradition means any teacher and any listeners, according to Bailey. But here is a very particular teacher and a very particular group of learners, in a strikingly special relationship.

Second, if the foundational source of the tradition is unique, then the teaching he gives—the content of the tradition—automatically takes on a special character and significance. Rainer Riesner draws attention to this point: "A word of Jesus was important not only because it could have been useful but also because it was the word of the messiah approved by God himself."[12] The material is not ordinary. The word "special" is hardly adequate. This is *a holy tradition*. The words of Jesus were of incalculable worth and importance.

As such, it would seem odd that the sayings of Jesus would have been entrusted to an uncontrolled and informal means of transmission. What fits perfectly the material and the master-disciple relationship of Jesus and the twelve is the model of the Pharisaic rabbi and disciples, where memorization was of a high importance.

Perhaps most importantly, the Jesus tradition as it is found in the gospels shows evidence of being designed for memorization. Riesner, who has studied the material thoroughly, concludes as follows: "According to my estimate, about 80 percent of the separate saying units

12. Rainer Riesner, "Jesus as Preacher and Teacher," in *Jesus and the Oral Gospel Tradition*, ed. Henry Wansbrough, JSNTSup 64 (Sheffield: Sheffield Academic Press, 1991), 209.

are formulated in some kind of *parallelismus membrorum*. To this one has to add other poetical techniques such as alliteration, assonance, rhythm and rhyme."[13] Does this point in the direction of an uncontrolled and informal transmission process that features endless variable performances? The very form of the material—as well as its content and its source—makes comparison with ordinary oral material and ordinary methods of transmission unhelpful.

The disciples function as "apostolic custodians" of the tradition. This does not look like an informal transmission, where there is not a set teacher or set students. This looks instead very much like a formal tradition—i.e., one where a specific teacher and specific disciples are in a special relationship, in which there are formal teaching and learning. All of this fits Gerhardsson's model (formal controlled tradition) far better than Bailey's model (informal controlled tradition).

We need finally to address the main objection to the proposal set forth by Gerhardsson. What is the perceived problem with the idea that behind Matthew, Mark, Luke, and John there was an oral tradition that is formal and controlled, along the lines of the transmission of the traditions of the Pharisees? The problem is that the reference to memorization seems incompatible with the differences that are encountered in the renderings of the teaching of Jesus in the Synoptic Gospels. If memory is

13. Riesner, "Jesus as Preacher and Teacher," 202. See Rainer Riesner, *Jesus als Lehrer: Eine Untersuchung zum Ursprung der Evangelien-Überlieferung*, 3rd ed., WUNT 2.7 (Tübingen: Mohr Siebeck, 1988), 392–404.

involved, it might seem that all the versions must agree verbatim. But we often encounter small differences. This is one of the places where Gerhardsson has been most misunderstood. From the beginning, he drew attention to the fact that minor variations are not incompatible with memorization. In fact, memorization does not prohibit variants, differences, adaptations, etc. Gerhardsson wrote *Memory and Manuscript* in part to correct the notion. There was of course "early work on the Christ-tradition," but it "seems to have taken place within fairly restricted limits, and thus to have had only limited freedom."[14] Yet, Gerhardsson does not deny the reality of that freedom and its impact upon the canonical gospels. It is furthermore clear that the variation in the transmission of the sayings of Jesus is much less than in the narrative materials. Only seldom in the Jesus tradition does one encounter halakic material; more often it is analogous to haggadic material, which the Pharisaic-rabbinic practice treated rather more freely. Gerhardsson readily admits that "the twelve and the other authoritative teachers . . . were not traditionists only. They worked with the Word. They worked on the Scriptures, and on the Christ-tradition (which was originally oral): they gathered, formulated (narrative tradition), interpreted, adapted, developed, complemented and put together collections for various definite purposes."[15]

Memorization, then, guarantees not every detail but the essence of the transmitted material. As Samuel

14. Gerhardsson, *Memory and Manuscript*, 44. See note 9 above.
15. Gerhardsson, *Memory and Manuscript*, 40.

Byrskog justly puts it: "The difference between the Gospels is no argument against the practice of memorization, as is often assumed, but shows that different people could choose to memorize the same thing in different ways and that memorization, while maintaining its distinctive preservative character, was never an entirely passive enterprise isolated from the social environment and activities of the larger group."[16] Once again, to quote Gerhardsson,

> Memorized texts need not be kept unaltered. I see memorization playing a basic role even when the wording is subject to some variation, particularly in the framework of the sayings and other narrative elements. Texts can also be memorized in more than one version. Textual variants are per se no argument against memorization: indeed, the alterations themselves can reveal a considerable retention of the wording.[17]

It is true, as some have pointed out, that the canonical gospels never report that Jesus taught by repetition to facilitate memorization. The authors of these texts can hardly be faulted for failing to point out something that would have been self-evident in that milieu.

Today, scholars tout their portrayal of "the real

16. Samuel Byrskog, "The Transmission of the Jesus Tradition," in *Handbook for the Study of the Historical Jesus*, ed. Tom Holmén and Stanley E. Porter (Leiden: Brill, 2011), 2:1465–94 (esp. 1487).

17. Birger Gerhardsson, "The Secret of the Transmission of the Unwritten Jesus Tradition," *NTS* 51 (2005): 1–18 (here 16).

Jesus" or the "historical Jesus." They throw grave doubt on the historical reliability of Matthew, Mark, Luke, and John. In such a climate, the argument of David Wenham's excellent book becomes very important. The underlying oral tradition provides the solid bedrock on which the canonical gospels depend, and by its very nature substantiates their trustworthiness.

DONALD A. HAGNER
George Eldon Ladd Professor Emeritus
of New Testament
Fuller Theological Seminary

Preface

Before the gospels were written, the first Christians passed on the good news of Jesus orally. Some scholars suppose that the process of preserving and passing on the stories and sayings of Jesus was informal and not very reliable; so many of the deeds and words ascribed to Jesus in the gospels are far removed from what the teacher of Galilee actually said and did. Others believe that the process was deliberate and the gospels rather reliable.[1] This book is not going to engage with those historical questions generally, but with one particular question: what did the very first Christians say about Jesus? Stated another way: what was their message when they went around the Mediterranean? This is an important question for anyone interested in the beginnings of Christianity, a question inadequately addressed by scholars.[2]

1. When I refer to "the gospels" in this book I will be referring to the canonical gospels (Matthew, Mark, Luke, and John), not to the other early Christian gospels.

2. My footnoting in this book is selective, focusing on the main

I am grateful to all those who have helped me with this book, including former colleagues and friends at Wycliffe Hall in Oxford and at Trinity College in Bristol, including John Nolland, J. Andrew Doole, Akio Ito, Travis Derico, Yongbom Lee, and Nathan Ridlehoover. Their collective comments on an early draft of the book, some suitably critical, were very valuable and have made this a better book. I also particularly appreciate the advice, encouragement and comments of my good friend of many years, Donald A. Hagner, and especially his willingness to write a substantial and relevant Foreword. I am grateful to Wm. B. Eerdmans Publishing Company for taking this book on and for all their help. As always, I am much indebted to my wife Clare for her support through the writing process and for her hard work on the bibliography and indices. The inspiration for this book came in part from the opportunity we had to visit Rome in 2013 and to take part in the international symposium on "The Gospels: Historical and Christological Research," sponsored by the Josef Ratzinger Foundation. I am grateful for the welcome extended by the organizers of the symposium and for the chance to revisit a city with so many associations with Peter and Paul, key figures in this book's discussion of how the first Christians proclaimed Jesus.

---

points being made. This is necessary, not least because the book touches on so many issues that have been debated at length by scholars. It would be impossible to do justice to them all in a book of this size. I have discussed in more detail some of the points that I note here in previous books, particularly on questions related to Paul and Jesus. This book draws on some of my earlier work, but the specific issue addressed in this book—the issues of the earliest oral tradition—is different, though related. Much of the argument is new.

Abbreviations

AB	Anchor Bible
ExpT	*Expository Times*
GE	The Brill Dictionary of Ancient Greek
JSNT	*Journal for the Study of the New Testament*
JSNTSup	Journal for the Study of the New Testament Supplement Series
NIGTC	New International Greek Testament Commentary
NTS	*New Testament Studies*
SJT	*Scottish Journal of Theology*
WUNT	Wissenschaftliche Untersuchungen zum Neuen Testament
ZTK	*Zeitschrift für Theologie und Kirche*

CHAPTER 1

Good News to Gospels

When the first Christians told people the good news of Jesus, what did they say? The new movement had an extraordinary impact. Beginning in Jerusalem around 31 CE, it spread like wildfire around the Roman Empire. There were riots in Rome itself by around 49 CE, which may have resulted from the arrival of the Christian movement.[1] Just ten years later Paul was writing a letter to an established and apparently vibrant church there.

But how did the young church have such success in a world with many religions on offer, in an Empire where worship of the Roman emperor was encouraged by the authorities, and in a context where a Galilean Jewish messiah was a very unlikely contender for allegiance? Scholars point to various sociological and spir-

---

1. Suetonius, a Roman historian, records that the Jews were expelled from Rome by Emperor Claudius because they were "rioting at the instigation of Chrestus," quite likely a reference to troubles in the Jewish community over the question of Jesus as "the Christ" (Suetonius, *Claud.* 25.4).

itual factors that made this new movement attractive. However, the evidence suggests that the most important thing was the distinctive message, the good news.[2] This message focused on Jesus of Nazareth. But what did they say about this unlikely person that captured the attention of so many in the ancient world?

They said that he had been crucified; that much is clear. No one would have invented the idea of a crucified messiah. Jesus's crucifixion is attested not only in the New Testament but also in Roman and Jewish sources.[3] There is nothing good or inspiring about someone being crucified. What transformed that rather sordid and unpleasant event for the Christians was the claim that Jesus came to life again. The Christian proclamation was that Jesus conquered death and that his death and resurrection were for the salvation of humankind.[4] So the first Christians went around the world inviting people

2. The canonical gospels speak of Jesus coming and "proclaiming" (e.g., Mark 1:14; 4:14; 6:12). Acts and the Epistles similarly portray the church as a proclaiming movement, with the "word" being central (e.g., Acts 1:22; 6:7, 8:5; Rom 10:15–18).

3. See the Roman historian Tacitus, *Ann.* 15.44, and also Jewish sources, e.g., b. Sanhedrin 43a, and possibly the much-debated Josephus, *A.J.* 18.63–64.

4. It is not easy to date some of the documents that make up the New Testament, but it is possible to be quite confident in dating some of Paul's letters, thanks to a combination of evidence from the New Testament itself and from archaeology (notably the evidence of Acts 18 and the Gallio inscription, which was discovered early in the twentieth century at Delphi in Greece and which enables us to date Paul's ministry in Corinth to 49–51 CE plus or minus a year). Paul's earliest letter is either the letter to the Galatians or 1 Thessalonians, with a date around 49 CE. What is striking is that in both letters the Christian message about Jesus as the Son of God—his death, resurrection, and expected return in the future—is taken for granted. It was already established Christian tradition.

to believe in this savior and to identify with him. So the movement spread.

That minimal account would not be contested by many serious historians, Christian or non-Christian.[5] But what else did the Christians say to persuade people about this Jesus?

It sometimes appears as though scholars believe that the very minimal gospel that we have outlined—Jesus was crucified and was raised from the dead for the salvation of the world—was all that the first Christians said or needed to say in order to convert people to faith in Jesus.[6] They point to some of the descriptions of the gospel that are found in the New Testament, such as 1 Cor 15:1–4 where Paul says: "I want you to know, brothers,[7] the gospel which I proclaimed to you . . . I passed on to you as of first importance what I also received that Christ died for our sins in accordance with the Scriptures, and that he was buried, and that he was raised on the third day in accordance with the Scriptures." This is indeed a

---

5. Of course, most non-Christians would not accept the claim that Jesus rose from the dead. A partial exception is Pinchas Lapide, *The Resurrection of Jesus: A Jewish Perspective* (London: SPCK, 1984). For accounts of Jesus by modern non-Christians, see, for example, Reza Aslan, *Zealot: The Life and Times of Jesus of Nazareth* (London: Westbourne, 2013), and Maurice Casey, *Jesus of Nazareth: An Independent Historian's Account of His Life and Teaching* (London: Black, 2002).

6. The ancient mystery religions celebrated a mythological story about the gods, although their attraction lay more in the salvation-bringing rituals than in the story. The Christian religion was quite different, with its story being about recent events that had taken place in a province of the Roman Empire.

7. I have translated literally. Paul's "brothers" should be understood to include "sisters."

succinct summary of the Christian good news, written in the 50s CE, reflecting both what Paul proclaimed in Corinth in the early 50s and very probably what he "received" when he became a believer in Jesus in the early 30s. But the references to the Scriptures are a very broad hint that there was much more to "the gospel" as Paul proclaimed and received it than simply a proclamation of Jesus's death and resurrection. The verses in 1 Cor 15 are a very brief summary of what Paul "passed on to them." In this section of the letter, Paul is addressing the question whether people rise from the dead or not. He reminds them of a few salient points from the gospel message, focusing his remarks on the resurrection.[8]

What is the fuller version of what Paul said about Jesus when he went from place to place, inviting people to believe in Jesus and to see him, rather than Caesar, as Lord of everything? What did people pass on to him when he became a Christian? What did Peter, the other apostles, and other less prominent evangelists say in those very early days?

The canonical gospels are usually dated between 50

8. It is possible to argue that 1 Cor 15:1–4 represents a particular perspective on the good news about Jesus, focusing on the death and resurrection of the Lord. Undoubtedly, there were other perspectives. Some likely focused on Jesus as a prophet or teacher. There is no doubt that Paul did have particular perspectives. Nevertheless, his summary is what he "received" from others at a very early date, and it was this message that had a huge impact on the world of the first century. The writers of the canonical gospels were very interested both in the teaching of the Lord and in his death and resurrection, so too was Paul, despite some contrary views. Whatever different emphases there may have been among the first Christians, all will have faced questions about Jesus when they proclaimed him as one to be believed and followed.

and 100 CE.[9] Most scholars believe that Mark was the first to be written, between 50 and 70 CE. Many think that there was also another written collection of sayings of Jesus, which Matthew and Luke both knew. This is referred to as Q.[10] This hypothetical document is usually dated to approximately 50 CE, or a little earlier. By this time, the church had been going strong for about twenty years, spreading across the Roman Empire. What did they tell people in the preceding "oral" period?

Scholars have often been surprisingly vague about this. Many suggest that in the early period there was no systematic preserving (or proclaiming) of the story of Jesus. Rather, early evangelists communicated occasional—and sometimes rather confused!—stories and sayings that happened to be remembered and were seen as relevant, a sort of religious folk-tradition. This is very roughly what many of the so-called form critics conclude on the basis of their analysis of the "form" of the stories. Yet, should one believe that when the earliest Christians came to places

9. But some date them even earlier, so James Bowman, *The Gospel of Mark: The New Christian Jewish Passover Haggadah* (Leiden: Brill, 1965), also John Wenham, *Redating Matthew, Mark and Luke* (London: Hodder, 1991), dating Matthew first.

10. From the German word *Quelle*, meaning "source." I will mostly refer to the "'two-source/two-document" hypothesis, although those who see Mark and Q as sources used by Matthew and Luke believe that Matthew and Luke also had additional sources of their own, often referred to as M and L. The two-source hypothesis thus becomes a four-source hypothesis. There is a sizable minority of scholars who do not subscribe to the two-source hypothesis, but to alternative theories, e.g., to the view that Luke knew and used Matthew as well as Mark. The main argument of this book applies to any literary theory of gospel origins, although the detailed interaction will mostly be with the two-document hypothesis.

and told people about Jesus they did not tell them very much about him? Would their hearers have been satisfied with minimal information or with a few striking tales and sayings but nothing more substantial or coherent?

It is certainly likely that one of the ways the "good news" got around was informally, one might say anecdotally. Matthew, Mark, Luke, and John themselves suggest that this happened in Jesus's lifetime. People met him and saw him in action. They told others about this extraordinary person. Those people, in turn, flocked to see and hear him. Something similar happened in the early days of the church's life, with people coming into contact with the enthusiastic and intriguing new movement of believers. Such informal sharing of news was a normal part of ancient communication. It may well have been impressively accurate, unlike some modern rumor and gossip.[11]

Although informal sharing of stories was very influential, that does not mean that people become followers of Jesus and adherents to his movement with very little knowledge about him. During the ministry of Jesus, they came to see for themselves and to listen to his teaching. After his ministry, people wanted to know about the

11. The work of Kenneth E. Bailey on what he calls "informally controlled oral tradition" in the Middle East has emphasized this (see his "Informal Controlled Oral Tradition and the Synoptic Gospels," *Themelios* 20 [1995]: 4–11). However, it is unlikely that the Christian tradition was only passed on in such an informal way. On this, see Michael Bird, *The Gospel of the Lord: How the Early Church Wrote the Story of Jesus* (Grand Rapids: Eerdmans, 2014), 74–124, and especially Travis Derico, *Oral Tradition and the Synoptic Verbal Agreement: Evaluating the Empirical Evidence for Literary Dependence* (Eugene, OR: Pickwick, 2016).

person the Christians were so enthusiastic about, before taking the big step of joining his movement.

Whatever else the first Christians were doing, they were trying to persuade people that the crucified Jesus was the Jewish messiah and a risen Lord, whom they needed to accept as savior from coming judgment. Such a message begs every question imaginable: Who was this person? Why was he crucified? What is the evidence that he came to life again? Why should one follow him? It is twenty-first-century arrogance to assume that people in the ancient world were wholly uncritical and would have swallowed any unlikely story about a crucified messiah. There were plenty of skeptics around during Jesus's ministry. This skepticism continued after his death. It must have been the case that the first Christians had to explain their enthusiasm for Jesus. So what did they say about him?

Scholars have examined the letters of Paul and other New Testament writings to see whether they can identify "early traditions." Some scholars identify "creedal" formulae, such as the summary of the gospel in 1 Cor 15 cited above. They have also suggested that some passages were early Christian hymns, such as the famous Phil 2:5–11, where Paul speaks of Jesus humbling himself even to the cross. These scholars assert that passages like 1 Cor 11:23–26—where Paul describes the Lord's Supper—were "liturgical texts." They also note occasional citations or echoes of Jesus's teaching, such as 1 Cor 7:10–11, where Paul paraphrases Jesus's teaching about divorce. But those suggestions hardly explain what Paul, Peter, or others proclaimed when they founded churches. There must have been something much more substantial than some basic creedal statements plus a few stories and sayings about someone who lived recently in Palestine. This Jewish-based movement could have made the huge impact that it did in the first-century world only if they had a strong, coherent, and persuasive message.

The simple argument of this short book is that there was regular and systematic teaching about Jesus, including about his life, teaching, death, and resurrection. The content of this teaching was a key part of the apologetic of the first Christians as they invited people to believe in "this Jesus," responded to the questions of outsiders, and taught people about "the way" of Jesus and about discipleship. The Christian faith has, from the very beginning, been a religion about history; to be more precise, Christians have claimed that God acted in history to reveal himself and to save the world through Jesus of Nazareth. For some religions, questions about historical origins are irrelevant. For Christianity, however, the historical person of Jesus matters and has always mattered. Telling his story cannot have begun when the gospels were written, but must have been at the heart of Christian mission from the beginning. Graham Stanton made this point well in his *Jesus of Nazareth in New Testament Preaching*, written forty years ago:

> It must have been all but impossible to avoid sketching out the life and character of Jesus in missionary proclaiming. How could one claim

that Jesus was the one person in the whole of history who fulfilled scripture in its widest and deepest sense, that Jesus was raised from the dead by God in a totally unexpected and unique way, and call for repentance and commitment to him without indicating who he was? How could one mention the crucifixion without answering in anticipation careful questioning about the events which led to the rejection of Jesus? Could one begin to mention the betrayal, arrest and trial of Jesus without arousing interest in the teachings and actions of Jesus?[12]

Arguments about what "must have been" the case in ancient history or ancient religion need to be used cautiously. It is all too easy to assume that "they then" viewed things as "I today" imagine them to have been. Is there evidence to support the existence of a substantial oral tradition of Jesus's life and teachings? This book argues in the affirmative.

My own interest in oral traditions of Jesus is not unique. Recently, there has been a wave of renewed interest in the question of oral tradition.[13] Various scholars

12. Graham N. Stanton, *Jesus of Nazareth in New Testament Preaching* (Cambridge: Cambridge University Press, 1974), 176–77.

13. There has been important study of ancient education with its emphasis on memorization. Scholars have debated the question of memory (and of how it works or does not work) both psychologically and socially. There have been a host of studies of different oral traditions, ancient and modern, from different parts of the world, which could in some ways be seen as parallel to the gospel traditions of Jesus. The recently revived interest in oral tradition might be said to have begun in Scandinavia with

have emphasized how important it is to take the oral tradition into account. So James D. G. Dunn in his notable presidential address to the international *Societas Novi Testamenti Studiorum* in 2002 spoke of changing "the Default Setting" in studies of the gospels, arguing forcefully and persuasively that oral tradition preceded and took precedence over literary accounts of Jesus for many years.[14]

Harald Riesenfeld, *The Gospel Tradition and Its Beginnings: A Study in the Limits of "Formgeschichte"* (London: Mowbray, 1957), and Birger Gerhardsson, *Memory and Manuscript: Oral Tradition and Written Transmission in Rabbinic Judaism and Early Christianity* (Lund: Gleerup, 1961). More recent contributions: Rainer Riesner, *Jesus als Lehrer: Eine Untersuchung zum Ursprung der Evangelien-Überlieferung*, WUNT 2.7 (Tübingen: Mohr Siebeck, 1981); Bo Reicke, *The Roots of the Synoptic Gospels* (Philadelphia: Fortress, 1986); Henry Wansborough, ed., *Jesus and the Oral Gospel Tradition* (Sheffield: JSOT, 1991); Werner Kelber, *The Oral and the Written Gospel: The Hermeneutics of Speaking and Writing in the Synoptic Tradition, Mark, Paul, and Q* (Bloomington: Indiana University Press, 1997); John Dominic Crossan, *The Birth of Christianity: Discovering What Happened in the Years Immediately after the Execution of Jesus* (Edinburgh: T&T Clark, 1999); Samuel Byrskog, *Story as History—History as Story: The Gospel Tradition in the Context of Ancient Oral History*, WUNT 123 (Tübingen: Mohr Siebeck, 2000); Armin Baum, *Der mündliche Faktor und seine Bedeutung für die synoptische Frage* (Tübingen: Francke, 2008); Robert K. McIver, *Memory, Jesus, and the Synoptic Gospels* (Atlanta: Society of Biblical Literature, 2011). Surveys of recent discussion include Eric Eve, *Behind the Gospels: Understanding the Oral Tradition* (London: SPCK, 2013); see also Derico, *Oral Tradition and the Synoptic Verbal Agreement*, who interacts critically with a wide range of discussions of oral tradition. Bird has a useful discussion in *Gospel of the Lord*, 74–124, as does Donald A. Hagner, *The New Testament: A Historical and Theological Introduction* (Grand Rapids: Baker, 2012), 106–16. Richard Bauckham, *Jesus and the Eyewitnesses*, 2nd ed. (Grand Rapids: Eerdmans, 2017);

14. Later published as James D. G. Dunn, "Altering the Default Setting: Re-envisaging the Early Transmission of the Jesus Tradition," *NTS* 49 (2003): 139–75. He has written extensively on oral tradition, including "social memory." See James D. G. Dunn, "Social Memory and the Oral Jesus Tradition," in *Memory in the Bible and Antiquity*, ed. Loren T. Stuckenbruck, Stephen C. Barton, and Benjamin G. Wold, WUNT 212 (Tübingen: Mohr Siebeck, 2007), 179–94. On social memory note also Chris Keith, "Memory and Authenticity: Jesus Tradition and What Really Happened," *ZNW* 102

Despite this recent interest, there has been surprisingly little attention given to the content of the earliest oral tradition. Even scholars who have fervently emphasized the importance of the oral tradition often seem to fail to carry that perception into their analysis and reading of the gospels.

The first part of the book, chapters 2–3, examines evidence suggesting the oral communication of traditions associated with Jesus goes back to Jesus himself, was seen as a priority by the earliest church, and is presupposed by the writers. "Teaching," "learning," "remembering," and "witnessing" are all key concepts. They point to the importance of passing on the oral traditions of Jesus. This is hardly surprising. Memorization played a crucial role in the cultural and educational contexts of Jesus and the first Christians. In chapter 4, and also in later chapters, I will examine the writings of Paul since he is a significant and datable witness both to the process of passing on Jesus traditions and to the shape and contents of the oral tradition before there were any written gospels.[15] Chap-

---

(2011): 155–77. See also James D. G. Dunn, *The Oral Gospel Tradition* (Grand Rapids: Eerdmans, 2013), and his magnum opus *Jesus Remembered*, vol. 1 of *Christianity in the Making* (Grand Rapids: Eerdmans, 2003), which reflects his emphasis on the importance of memory in the transmission of Jesus traditions.

15. I could have looked also at the non-Pauline letters of the New Testament and Revelation. These texts offer further evidence for the use of oral tradition about Jesus, such as the echoes of the Sermon on the Mount in the letters of James and 1 Peter. I could also have examined other evidence for the ongoing importance of the oral tradition, including Papias's comment on preferring the "living" voice to the written sources (Eusebius, *Hist. eccl.* 3.39.4). On this evidence see among others Donald A. Hagner, "The Sayings of Jesus in the Apostolic Fathers and Justin Martyr,"

ters 5 and 6 show how an appreciation of oral tradition makes more sense of various features in the gospels than purely literary explanations. Chapters 7 and 8 complete the argument, making further observations about the extent and form of the oral tradition and discussing some of the implications and issues raised by the thesis of the book. My thesis is that oral tradition was indeed the default setting. Further, the oral tradition was substantial and carefully preserved.[16]

---

in *The Jesus Tradition outside the Gospels*, ed. David Wenham, vol. 5 of *Gospel Perspectives* (Sheffield: JSOT, 1985), 233–68.

16. Changing default settings can be very easy on a computer, but very difficult in the world of ideas or scholarly debate. It is difficult for people to see things differently, especially when they and many others have worked for a long time with particular theories or paradigms, often with quite good results (or so it seems). There is an understandable academic inertia with a dominant hypothesis (e.g., the two-document hypothesis) gathering momentum and power as more and more people support it. It is common for research students (and others) to say "for the purpose of this thesis I will be assuming the two-document hypothesis as the probable solution of the Synoptic problem." As a result, more and more work is done from one angle and with one set of presuppositions. Alternative views are poorly represented in the academic market and commentaries. They are often quickly dismissed or just ignored. (See on this the remarks of William R. Farmer, *The Synoptic Problem: A Critical Analysis* [Macon: Mercer University, 1976], 178–98.) This might not matter if the dominant hypothesis were completely and certainly correct, though even in that case it could operate as a straightjacket inhibiting fresh perspectives. But the two-document hypothesis is not "completely and certainly" correct, as the trickle of dissenting scholars—whether advocates of Matthean priority, disbelievers in Q, or advocates of oral theories—makes clear. The stranglehold of one hypothesis prevents progress and blinds readers to potentially fruitful readings of other texts. In supporting the call for a changed default setting, this book is not calling for or advocating a radically different solution to the Synoptic problem or for the abandonment of all literary explanations of the problem. Rather, it is an argument for the affirmation of the priority of oral tradition in earliest Christianity and for the view that there were strong and substantial traditions about Jesus.

CHAPTER 2

The Teaching of Jesus and the Story of Acts

Jesus was a teacher, and his disciples were learners (the root meaning of the Greek word for "disciple" is learner).[1] The importance of Jesus as a teacher is clear from all the gospels. Mark includes the least amount of Jesus's teaching. However, the author of Mark goes out of his way to emphasize Jesus's teaching and his authority as a teacher (e.g., 1:22; 4:1–2). The other canonical gospels are no different in terms of this emphasis. They devote much of their accounts to his teaching.

In the modern world, books are widely available. Note-taking and writing are common. Computers are our constant companions. In Jesus's day, some people were literate. There were professional writers (or scribes). However, it was largely an oral culture; most people learned by listening and learning. The good teacher taught so

---

1. Although the portrayal of Jesus and his disciples in the gospels is often discussed, there is no real doubt that he did teach and did have disciples.

that the content would be memorable and easy to retain. Birger Gerhardsson has demonstrated how careful and effective the teaching of Jewish rabbis typically was, with traditions being "received" and "passed on" (to quote the language of Paul).[2] Jesus was not a formally trained rabbi who taught in the context of a scribal school. Rather, he was more of a prophet.[3] Even as a prophet, he would have wanted his message taken to heart, not forgotten. Many have noted that the sayings of Jesus have been shaped to be memorable, almost poetic. If there is every reason to think that Jesus taught in a way that could be remembered, there is also every reason to believe that his disciples would have been good learners.[4]

Furthermore, according to the gospels, Jesus sent his disciples out as itinerant missionaries to continue his work of proclaiming the kingdom of God, as well as teaching and healing.[5] They would have gone out with a

2. Birger Gerhardsson, *Memory and Manuscript: Oral Tradition and Written Transmission in Rabbinic Judaism and Early Christianity*, 3rd ed. (Grand Rapids: Eerdmans, 1998). Gerhardsson has critics. Yet, his general points about the culture remain important. For clarification of his ideas, see Birger Gerhardsson, *The Reliability of the Gospel Tradition* (Peabody, MA: Hendrickson, 2001). See also Baum, *Der mündliche Faktor und seine Bedeutung für die synoptische Frage*.

3. Jesus was sometimes scathing about the scribes and their misleading teaching. But Matthew describes a positive parable about "a scribe discipled for the kingdom of heaven" (Matt 13:52). Jesus was addressed by people as "teacher" or even "rabbi" (e.g., Mark 10:17; 14:45).

4. See especially on this Riesner, *Jesus als Lehrer*. An English edition of Riesner is planned. See also Rainer Riesner, "Jesus as Preacher and Teacher," in *Jesus and the Oral Gospel Tradition*, ed. Henry Wansbrough (Sheffield: JSOT, 1991), 185–210.

5. An "apostle" is someone sent, and often someone sent as a representative of the one sending. This practice is broadly attested in all three

message about Jesus and his ministry. It is reasonable to suppose that they prepared carefully. They would have learned from Jesus what to say and how to say it. Indeed the "mission discourse" in Matt 10 (and in Mark 6 and Luke 9) may be seen as a sort of briefing of them by Jesus, although it is, of course, a summary and they would not simply have told people that "the kingdom of God has come near." They would have said much more and told people about Jesus and who he was. So the process of "passing on" what we might call "Jesus tradition" began during Jesus's ministry itself.[6]

If that is the case, then it is wholly probable (if not inevitable) that the same pattern of teaching and learning was at the heart of the disciples' proclaiming of the good news after Jesus had left them. Of course, for them the death and resurrection of Jesus would come to be the primary story, not just Jesus's teaching about the kingdom of God.[7]

The writer of the Acts of the Apostles affirms that this is exactly what happened when the first Christians began to take their good news to the world. Acts was written by the same person as Luke's Gospel, as is made quite explicit in the opening words of the book, where the author refers to "my first volume" (Acts 1:1). Acts is a very important document, being our only account of

---

of the Synoptic Gospels. It is also indirectly affirmed by Paul in 1 Cor 9 and other texts.

6. So Bird, *The Gospel of the Lord*, 89.

7. Even during Jesus's ministry the disciples certainly told people about Jesus when they went out on mission and proclaimed the kingdom.

the earliest Christian church. Despite debates about its reliability, it certainly contains historical information and needs to be taken seriously.

Luke (we use the traditional name) makes it clear from the first chapter of Acts onward that remembering and telling the story of Jesus was a top priority in the first Christian church—understandably now that Jesus had left them. In Acts 1, a successor to Judas Iscariot is chosen to fill the gap left in the group of twelve apostles following his betrayal of Jesus and subsequent death. Peter very specifically says that to be eligible the one chosen must be "one of the men who accompanied us all the time that the Lord Jesus came in and went out among us, beginning from the baptism of John until the day when he was taken up from us—one of these must become a witness to his resurrection with us" (vv. 21–22). The role of the twelve in this passage is explicitly defined as being a witness to Jesus, and, although they will have a much wider leadership role in the church than simply transmitting tradition, Acts repeatedly emphasizes the themes of witness and of the teaching from the apostles (2:32, 42; 3:15; 6:2–4; 10:39). The main focus of their witness is to the fact that Jesus had risen from the dead. However, the qualification for being one of the twelve is not just seeing the risen Jesus, but also having been with him during his ministry. The implication is that it was their task to tell people the whole story of Jesus—from his baptism to his ascension, including his teaching.[8]

8. Acts 20:35 is a particularly intriguing reference to "remembering" traditions of Jesus, since the saying does not appear in any of the gospels:

Luke tells us in Acts what the first Christians said when they told people the good news of Jesus. The center of the message was the story of Jesus; it is the focus in the very first speech (Acts 2), and consistently throughout the book. Of course, Acts—rather like Paul in his letters—gives us only short extracts from the speeches of the early Christians, often bringing out the application to the particular audience. Some speeches touch upon the Old Testament background to Jesus. Others emphasize the folly of idols when speaking to Gentiles (e.g., Acts 13 and 14). However, the focus of the speeches rests on Jesus and his resurrection.

Most instructive for our discussion is Peter's proclamation to the Gentile centurion Cornelius and family in Acts 10:36–43. Here, Peter is addressing people who lived in Joppa (modern Jaffa) on the Mediterranean coast, not in Jerusalem or in Galilee (where Jesus was relatively well-known). Peter says:

> As for the word that he sent to the sons of Israel, proclaiming good news of peace through Jesus Christ (he is Lord of all), you know the story of what happened throughout all Judea, beginning from Galilee after the baptism that John

---

"it is necessary for us to help the weak and to remember the words of the Lord Jesus how he himself said, 'It is more blessed to give than to receive.'" Of course, the Lukan portrayal of the witnessing and teaching role of the apostles could be seen as Christian apologetic lending weight to the Christian message. It probably does serve that function. However, that does not mean that it is without historical basis. It certainly receives some support from Paul's comments on apostleship in his letters.

proclaimed: the story of Jesus of Nazareth, how God anointed him with the Holy Spirit and with power. He went about doing good and healing all who were oppressed by the devil, for God was with him. And we are witnesses of all the things that he did both in the country of the Jews and in Jerusalem. They put him to death, hanging him from a tree. This one God raised on the third day and made him appear, not to all the people but to witnesses who had been chosen by God, to us, who ate and drank with him after he rose from the dead. And he commanded us to proclaim to the people and to testify that he is the one appointed by God as judge of the living and the dead. To this one all the prophets bear witness that everyone who believes in him receives forgiveness of sins through his name.

Here one notes that Luke's summary of the good news as shared with Cornelius and family is a summary of the story of Jesus, not dissimilar to what is found in the canonical gospels (esp. Mark).[9]

9. It could be argued that the Cornelius story is the only example of the first Christians narrating the full story of Jesus in this way and that none of the other evangelistic proclamation described in Acts has this narrative shape. Although there are no other examples of such an extensive telling of the story, most if not all of the evangelistic proclaiming does focus in some way on the story, notably on the death and resurrection of Jesus. The fact that it is not so extensively told as with Cornelius is easily explained: Luke is only giving very brief summaries of the proclamation and teaching. He naturally focuses on the most important part of the narrative (i.e., the death and resurrection), as well as on the links that the

A similarly important piece of evidence about what the first Christians said is the very last verse of Acts, where Luke refers to Paul living under house arrest in Rome. He says that Paul "welcomed all who came to him, proclaiming the kingdom of God and teaching about the Lord Jesus Christ with all boldness and without hindrance" (28:30, 31). What is especially striking here is the reference to "the kingdom of God," as this is the dominant theme of Jesus's teaching in the Synoptic Gospels. This together with "teaching about the Lord Jesus Christ" tells us that Paul's proclaiming of the gospel, according to the author of Acts, was telling people about Jesus and his teaching.

It is hardly surprising that Luke, for whom Paul was a hero and (probably) colleague, tells us that Paul's ministry had this focus, because Luke himself had written his account before the book of Acts. And Luke saw his account as telling the story of Jesus very much in the same way as the story was told when the good news of Jesus was proclaimed in the first days of the church. This comes

---

preacher made with their audiences, whether Jewish or Gentile. There are other things that may help explain the infrequent references back to Jesus's ministry in the evangelistic proclamation of Acts. In the very earliest days of outreach in Jerusalem and Judea, emphasis was necessarily on explaining the death and proclaiming the resurrection of Jesus. Even with Cornelius and family who have lived in Judea for some time, Peter can say, "*You know* what has happened throughout Judea, beginning in Galilee." In this case, Peter reminds them of the story. On this, see Christoph W. Stenschke, "The Jewish Savior for Israel in the Missionary Speeches of Acts," in *The Earliest Perceptions of Jesus in Context: Essays in Honour of John Nolland*, ed. A. W. White, David Wenham, and Craig A. Evans (London: T&T Clark, forthcoming). Luke does not need to narrate the story of Jesus in Acts; he had written the Gospel. The author does presuppose that the first Christians told the story to people who were unfamiliar with it.

out in Luke 1:1–4, the prologue, where Luke addresses himself to one Theophilus. We do not know who Theophilus was. Yet, two important points are worthy of note: first, Luke says that he has written his account of Jesus "so that you may know the reliability (Greek: *asphaleian*) of the things you have been taught (Greek: *katēchēthēs*)." The clear implication is that Theophilus, on becoming a Christian, had been taught about Jesus; Luke thinks he can improve on what Theophilus has learned.[10]

Second, in describing how he has written his account, Luke specifically speaks of "things that have been fulfilled among us, as they were handed on to us by those who were eyewitnesses and servants of the word from the beginning"; that phraseology is the sort of language used to describe the apostles in Acts (1:21, 22; 6:4). Luke is claiming that his account is based on the eyewitness testimony especially associated with the apostles. Luke is doing exactly what they and other Christian teachers did—telling people about Jesus, his teaching, life, death, resurrection, and ascension. In other words, the Gospel of Luke is the message that was regularly proclaimed by the followers of Jesus.[11]

---

10. Even if Theophilus is a pseudonym (as some think), the point remains that Luke presupposes a process of teaching in the church.

11. The emphasis in Acts 1 on the apostolic testimony to Jesus can be seen as a link back to the Gospel of Luke, both in a historical and literary sense. Historically, it was important after the departure of Jesus to have his story preserved and retold. From a literary perspective, the reference to the apostolic testimony is one of the things that connects Acts to the Gospel. The story of Luke's Gospel is what the early followers communicated to the world in their mission as described in the book of Acts. So also Stenschke, "The Jewish Savior."

So three things from Luke's writings—his description of the twelve apostles and their role, his description of the first Christians' proclaiming, and his explanation of his own gospel writing—all indicate that the first Christians told the story of Jesus.

Before leaving the evidence of Luke, a word on the hitorical reliability of Acts is in order. Is Luke's account of what they did in the earliest days of the church to be believed? Might it not be that he has crafted his accounts to give them credibility as semi-apostolic? Up to a point, this is quite probably the case and is implied in his prologue. However, that does not mean that he is reading back his own historical or quasi-historical interests into the story in a way that reflects his interests rather than what actually happened? Certainly, some scholars have seen Acts more as a Lukan novel than as well-informed history.[12]

However, though there are some questions about Luke's historical accuracy,[13] there is reason to think that Acts contains plenty of good history. The prologue (Luke 1:1–4) shows us an author who purports to be giving a careful and well-researched account. It could be a formal opening, without any substance. However, the author does proceed in a way that suggests a real interest in setting his account of Jesus in the real historical Roman world (for example, see 3:1–3).[14]

---

12. Notably Richard I. Pervo, *Acts: A Commentary*, Hermeneia (Philadelphia: Fortress, 2009).

13. E.g., there are the references to Quirinius (Luke 2:1–3) as well as Theudas and Judas (Acts 5:35–37). Even they show Luke's interest in history.

14. On the prologue, see especially Loveday Alexander, *The Preface*

The main arguments for the historical unreliability of Acts have to do with his accounts of Paul, which are seen as at odds with Paul's accounts of himself and his ministry. Acts is thought to have made Paul less radical and to have confusing information about his life. It is not possible to explore this issue in detail here.[15] But these arguments are more tenuous than is often thought.[16] Most

---

to Luke's Gospel: Literary Convention and Social Context in Luke 1:1–4 and Acts 1.1 (Cambridge: Cambridge University Press, 2005).

15. I explored the question of Paul in Acts at some length in David Wenham, "Acts and the Pauline Corpus II. The Evidence of Parallels," in *Ancient Literary Setting*, ed. Bruce W. Winter and Andrew D. Clarke, vol. 1 of *The Book of Acts in Its First Century Setting* (Grand Rapids: Eerdmans, 1993), 215–58. Cf. David Wenham, *Paul and Jesus: The True Story* (London: SPCK, 2002). Others have explored the question in more detail. See Colin Hemer, *The Book of Acts in the Context of Hellenistic History* (Winona Lakes: Eisenbrauns, 1989); Rainer Riesner, *Paul's Early Period: Chronology, Mission Strategy, Theology* (Grand Rapids: Eerdmans, 1998); Craig Keener, *Acts: An Exegetical Commentary*, 4 vols. (Grand Rapids: Baker, 2012–2015).

16. One of the much debated questions relating to the reliability of Acts relates to his references to Paul's visits to Jerusalem following his conversion, as compared to those in Paul's letters and especially Galatians. Acts has Paul go up to Jerusalem three times: (1) shortly after this conversion (Acts 9:2–28), (2) on a mercy mission in time of famine (Acts 11:27–29), and (3) to discuss problems over the Gentile mission (Acts 15). Paul, on the other hand, in Gal 2 seems to be detailing his post-conversion visits carefully, and has no reference (apparently) to the famine relief visit. The second visit that he describes is a discussion of the Gentile mission with church leaders. It sounds more like Luke's third visit. So Luke is often thought to have invented his second visit or to have been quite confused. This conclusion is, however, unwarranted. Paul's second visit according to Acts (the famine relief visit) occurs after a period described in Acts (11:22–26) when Paul has been working with Barnabas in leading the church in Antioch, the hugely important capital city of the Roman province of Syria (modern Antakya). The notable and controversial thing about this church is that it was, according to Acts, the first church to include a number of uncircumcised Gentile converts, potentially a very worrying situation for the Jewish Christians of Jerusalem. They accordingly sent Barnabas down, according to Acts, to supervise the situation. He approved what was going

of Luke's history works remarkably well. One example of this is his account of Paul's ministry at Corinth in Acts. The reference to the expulsion of the Jews from Rome in 18:2 has a supportive parallel in Suetonius's life of Claudius. Further, his reference to the governor of Achaia, Gallio, fits with the famous Gallio inscription.[17] There are

---

on and later went on to bring outsider Paul to help lead the church. This is the context within the book of Acts for the famine relief visit to Jerusalem by Paul and Barnabas. Acts does not describe any discussions that were had. Despite this silence, it is unthinkable that Paul and Barnabas would not have had serious discussions with church leaders in Jerusalem about their ministry in Antioch. This is exactly what Galatians suggests happened for Paul's second visit. The narrative reports that the leaders in Jerusalem gave Barnabas and Paul (who was still suspect to some in Jerusalem) the "right hand of fellowship" to go to the Gentiles, Gal 2:1–10. Far from not fitting, Acts and Galatians fit extremely well. Alternative historical reconstructions do not work as well.

17. Suetonius, *Claud.* 25.4. Another interesting convergence of evidence related to Acts 18 involves 1 Thess 2:16, where Paul speaks of Jewish opposition to the gospel and then of "God's wrath coming on them at last." This has perplexed commentators, with some concluding that it is a scribal gloss added after the destruction of Jerusalem in 70 CE. But Paul is likely writing 1 Thessalonians from Corinth, where he recently arrived. He is probably staying at the home of Aquila and Priscilla, who recently arrived from Rome after the great expulsion of the Jews from Rome by Emperor Claudius. Such an event could very easily have been seen by Paul as a sign of God's wrath on the Jews. This likelihood increases if Paul had heard of the terrible massacre by Roman soldiers of thousands of Jews in Jerusalem (cf. Josephus, *B.J.* 9.223–31), which happened in the same year as the expulsion (49 CE). On this, see Ernst Bammel, "Judenverfolgung und Naherwartung. Zur Eschatologie des ersten Thessalonicherbriefs," *ZTK* 56 (1959): 294–315, and David Wenham, *Paul: Follower of Jesus or Founder of Christianity?* (Grand Rapids: Eerdmans, 1995), 299–301. Carol J. Schlueter, *Filling up the Measure: Polemical Hyperbole in 1 Thessalonians 2:14–16* (Sheffield, JSOT: 1994), 94–95, 106, agrees that Paul must have an external event, a "large disaster," in mind. However, she thinks it is impossible to tell what it was. Schlueter mentions Bammel's argument. She fails to align Acts with 1 Thess 2:17 to see the full significance of the fact that Paul is writing the letter shortly after the expulsion of the Jews from Rome. According

numerous examples in Acts in which factual and topographical details are right (e.g., identifying local officials whom Paul and his party met and giving them their correct titles [13:7; 16:22; 17:6; 18:12; 19:31; 28:7]).[18] Acts is not a novel. Rather, it is well-informed history.

This is hardly surprising, if the evidence of the "we" passages in Acts is taken at face value. Luke's use of the first person in the narrative from Acts 16:10 onward is most naturally taken to mean that the author was with Paul on his journeys.[19] Some scholars have suggested other explanations (e.g., the author was using someone else's diary or using the first person for dramatic effect). Yet, these suggestions carry serious weight only if Acts is deemed unreliable on other grounds and is therefore unlikely to come from one of Paul's companions. In fact, he is repeatedly and demonstrably reliable. There is no cogent case for questioning the very early tradition that the author was a companion of Paul, who was with him when he went to Jerusalem for the last time and apparently throughout his years of imprisonment first in Jerusalem, then in Caesarea, and then in Rome.[20]

---

to Acts 18:2, Paul was staying and working with people who had recently experienced the trauma of the Claudian expulsion.

18. See Hemer, *Acts*, 101–243.

19. The "we" references come and go in an unsystematic way. On the "we" passages, see the detailed and authoritative work by Claus-Jürgen Thornton, *Der Zeuge des Zeugen Lukas als Historiker der Paulusreisen*, WUNT 56 (Tübingen: Mohr Siebeck, 1991). His conclusion is that Luke's "view of the history comes for him straight out of experience of it . . . he gets his perception through his eyes" (367, my literal translation).

20. The accounts of Paul's defenses and trials in Acts 22–26 are almost tediously repetitive (repeating the account in Acts 9). Yet, this account along with the references to the governors Felix and Festus (with

If this is correct, Luke was in Palestine.[21] He would have had ample opportunity to pursue the research that he mentions in the prologue. Further, Luke would have been able to interview and get to know eyewitnesses of Jesus's life and ministry (including members of Jesus's family, such as his brother, James, who succeeded Peter as leader of the Jerusalem church). [22]

All of this lends credibility to Luke's account, both of Jesus and of the early church, and to his account of the preaching of the earliest church, in which telling the story of Jesus was a key part. This is not to say that Luke was not a serious literary artist. He was a theologian and creative writer. Luke not only reproduced the traditions that he received and heard. He also arranged those traditions to address questions that Theophilus and others may have had. But Luke was not a novelist, telling tales. Rather, he was someone trying to give a reliable account of Jesus and the movement that followed, bringing out the meaning and significance of the story as he saw it.

If that positive conclusion about the "we" passages and Acts as a whole seems to some too historically optimistic, the alternative is not necessarily to discount the

---

Agrippa and Bernice) suggests an account that is historically based, not invented. The shipwreck narrative of Acts 27 is a remarkable account of an ancient sea voyage; see Brian M. Rapske, "Acts, Travel and Shipwreck," in *The Book of Acts in Its Graeco-Roman Setting*, ed. David W. J. Gill and Conrad Gempf, vol. 2 of *The Book of Acts in Its First Century Setting* (Grand Rapids: Eerdmans 1994), 1–47.

21. I am using the term Palestine in its academic sense, i.e., to refer to ancient Judea, Samaria, and Galilee, not in its modern political sense.

22. This would be the case, even if Luke was absent for some of the time during those years.

evidence of Acts completely or to deny that there may be truth in what Acts describes, including about the early Christian proclamation of Jesus. Acts is on any account our earliest record and primary source for the earliest history of the church. It is an important witness to the unsurprising view that the first Christians told the story of Jesus.

CHAPTER 3

The Evidence of Mark, Matthew, and John

The view that the first Christians told the story of Jesus when evangelizing their world is explicit in Acts. The author of Acts envisions his account, the Gospel of Luke, in that way. The writers of Matthew, Mark, Luke, and John claim, indirectly at least, that their narratives are versions of the good news of Jesus, accounts of what Jesus wanted his disciples to pass on.

Mark is usually seen by scholars as the earliest of the four canonical gospels. Very ancient testimony (going back to the early second century) points to John Mark being the author and to the Gospel of Mark being an account of Peter's proclamation of Jesus.[1] If that was the case (and there is a good case in support), it is significant for the argumeny here, given Peter's priority in the earliest days of the church.[2]

1. Traditionally identified with the Mark of Acts 12:12; 15:39; Col 4:10; Phlm 24; 1 Pet 5:13.
2. This view has been defended and expounded in Richard Bauckham, *Jesus and the Eyewitnesses*, 2nd ed. (Grand Rapids: Eerdmans, 2017). The new

Mark begins with "The beginning of the *good news* of Jesus Christ (the Son of God)." It is not necessary for our

---

edition responds to critiques of the first edition (2006). For critiques, see Jens Schröter, "The Gospels as Eyewitness Testimony? A Critical Examination of Richard Bauckham's Jesus and the Eyewitnesses," *JSNT* 31 (2008): 195–209, and Craig A. Evans, "The Implications of Eyewitness Tradition," *JSNT* 31.2 (2008): 211–19. See also the response: Richard Bauckham, "Eyewitnesses and Critical History: A Response to Jens Schröter and Craig Evans," *JSNT* 31.2 (2008): 221–35. Note also Samuel Byrskog, "The Eyewitnesses as Interpreters of the Past: Reflections on Richard Bauckham's Jesus and the Eyewitnesses," *Journal for the Study of the Historical Jesus* 6 (2008): 157–68; David Catchpole, "On Proving Too Much: Critical Hesitations about Richard Bauckham's Jesus and the Eyewitnesses," *Journal for the Study of the Historical Jesus* 6 (2008): 169–81; I. Howard Marshall, "A New Consensus on Oral Tradition? A Review of Richard Bauckham's Jesus and the Eyewitnesses," *Journal for the Study of the Historical Jesus* 6 (2008): 182–93; Stephen J. Patterson, "Can You Trust a Gospel? A Review of Richard Bauckham's Jesus and the Eyewitnesses," *Journal for the Study of the Historical Jesus* 6 (2008): 194–210; Theodore J. Weeden, "Polemics as a Case for Dissent: A Response to Richard Bauckham's Jesus and the Eyewitnesses," *Journal for the Study of the Historical Jesus* 6 (2008): 211–24. See also the response: Richard Bauckham, "In Response to My Respondents: Jesus and the Eyewitnesses in Review," *Journal for the Study of the Historical Jesus* 6 (2008): 225–53. The association of Peter with Mark has been defended by other scholars, notably by Martin Hengel, *The Four Gospels and the One Gospel of Jesus Christ* (London: SCM, 2000), 34–115. One example of a feature in Mark that tells in favor of Mark being based on eyewitness testimony is the reference in Mark 15:22 to Simon of Cyrene (in North Africa) being forced to carry the cross of Jesus. Mark identifies Simon as the "father of Alexander and Rufus." The obvious question is: Who are Alexander and Rufus? They are not involved in the story. It seems likely that they were people who were known to the author of Mark and his readers. If that is the case, it shows that the writer had contacts with people who possessed first-hand knowledge of the events. The popular idea that the young man who ran away naked in Mark 14:51–52 was Mark is as good an explanation of that text as any, although there is no way of proving it. In any case, it is plausibly seen as "a historical reminiscence, especially memorable to a member of Mark's intended audience," so Kim Huat Tan, *Mark: A New Covenant Commentary* (Cambridge: Lutterworth, 2016), 201. If Mark was indeed the author, our question remains unanswered: "What did the first Christians say about Jesus when proclaiming the good news?" Yet, Mark's authorship does help close the historical gap between the writer and the Gospel of Mark.

purposes to go into all the textual questions—is "the Son of God" part of the original text of Mark?—nor even into the question of what Mark means exactly when he says "The beginning of the good news." What is important to bear in mind is that the word *euangelion*, when used by Mark, does not have the modern sense of a written document about Jesus. Mark uses the word in the sense that Paul and other texts in the New Testament use it, i.e., to refer to the Christian good news of Jesus, the message believed and proclaimed by the early church.[3] Yet, the author of Mark here helps create a new meaning for *euangelion*, a written account of Jesus's life.

Mark sees what he is writing as embodying this good news, as he makes clear. He thus confirms to us that in his view the good news of Jesus, proclaimed by the church, is the story of Jesus, such as he is about to tell us in the document that follows.

We also notice two other things in Mark both to do with his disciples: first, when Jesus calls Peter, his fishermen friends, and later the tax-collector Levi (1:17, 2:14) to become his disciples, the invitation is to "follow me." Discipleship in the Gospel of Mark is more than anything else "following Jesus," including the journey to the cross

---

3. This is how he uses the word himself later in Mark (e.g., 1:14; 13:10). The word has for the New Testament authors a secular and an Old Testament background. For example, Isa 52:7 speaks of the beautiful feet of the one bringing good news. In the age before modern communications it was a herald who would come to a town or village and announce the news, hopefully joyful news, e.g., of peace. So too, Jesus announces "the kingdom of God has come near." Jesus does not just announce this; rather, he enacts it. See Bird, *The Gospel of the Lord*, 5–20.

(8:34). In the Markan narrative the disciples are able to follow very literally, going with Jesus, finally up to Jerusalem where Jesus is crucified and raised from the dead. It is not spelled out, but there can be little question that Mark would see this calling to follow as a continuing call to Christian disciples (8:34). But how can it be done, for those who are not first-generation followers? It is likely that Mark sees his account of Jesus and his disciples as enabling his readers also to see, to hear, and to follow Jesus. Passing on the story of Jesus is an essential part of making and training disciples.

Secondly, the twelve in Mark are appointed to be "with Jesus." Then, they go out and do as Jesus has done: proclaim the good news of the kingdom, cast out demons, and heal. It is not hard to deduce that Mark (rather like Luke in Acts 1) sees the disciples as informed witnesses who will take the teaching of Jesus to the world (13:10).

It is perhaps less easy to show this with Matthew, seen by most scholars as being dependent on Mark. And yet Matthew concludes with the risen Jesus in all his authority commissioning those who are with him to "go then and make disciples of all the nations, baptizing them . . . *and teaching them to keep all that I commanded you*" (28:16–20). For Matthew discipleship of Jesus entails following, as in Mark, but also and especially obeying the teaching of Jesus. This comes out also in the conclusion to the Sermon on the Mount with the stress on keeping Jesus's words (7:24–27).

The way people will learn these commands and words is through the disciples whom Jesus sends out to teach. It has often been observed that Matthew portrays the disciples more positively than Mark.[4] This has sometimes been seen as his whitewashing of church leaders. If so, he does not do a very good job.[5] Much more likely, his portrayal of the disciples as people who do succeed in learning from Jesus, even if slowly, is connected with his emphasis on their future role as evangelist-teachers who are going to pass on the teaching of Jesus (28:16–20). Matthew quite clearly sees his narrative as doing just that. For him becoming a disciple involves learning (and then obeying) Jesus's teaching, and also no doubt learning about the deeds and person of Jesus. Passing on the story and sayings of Jesus is at the heart of making disciples, and at the heart of Matthew's purpose in writing his gospel.

Finally, what about the Fourth Gospel? There are many questions about John and its relationship to Matthew, Mark, and Luke. It is quite distinctive and has often been judged to be more theological and less historical than the Synoptic Gospels. There probably is something in that view. At the same time, there is evidence to show (1) that John has historical information about Jesus that the others do not record[6] and (2) that John also sees his

---

4. E.g., compare Mark 4:10 with Matt 13:51. Compare also Mark 6:51–52 with Matt 14:33.

5. They struggle in Matthew as well: e.g., in Matt 16:17–20 Peter is congratulated for his understanding by Jesus, but three or so verses later his failure to understand Jesus's prediction of his suffering results in a rebuke: "Get behind me, Satan! You are an offense to me."

6. There are interesting ingredients in John that have a claim to being historical, e.g., his account of Jesus working for a time in Judea alongside John the Baptist almost as John's disciple (chs. 3–4), the healing of the lame man at the pool of Bethesda (5:2), his reference to Jesus going

account as telling the story of Jesus so that people may believe in Jesus.

At the end of chapter 20—which may well have been the original conclusion—he specifically explains what he has been doing. He refers to the many "signs" that Jesus accomplished and comments "these are written that you may believe that Jesus is the Christ the Son of God and believing you may have life in his name" (vv. 30–31). There is debate over the Greek word used in the phrase "that you may believe." Does it suggest "come to believe" or "go on believing"? It is not possible to be certain. Perhaps John meant both? Either way, it should be noted that John sees telling the story of Jesus as the way to help people in belief.

John has selected his stories and told them in such a way as to facilitate belief. The story immediately preceding John's statement of intent is that of Thomas who struggles to believe that Jesus is alive. After all, dead men do not come back to life! But, Thomas sees Jesus, is convinced, and says movingly "My Lord and my God" (20:26–28). John then goes on to say that he has written to help readers believe. Between the story about Thomas and John's statement of intent is a saying of Jesus: "Have you believed because you have seen me? Blessed are those who have not seen and yet have believed" (20:29). This

---

to Jerusalem several times, and his description of Jesus's "new commandment" (13:34, see discussion of Gal 6:2 and 5:13 in ch. 5 below). On John and history see, among many other recent discussions, John Lierman, ed., *Challenging Perspectives on the Gospel of John*, WUNT 2.219 (Tübingen: Mohr Siebeck, 2006), and Richard Bauckham, *The Testimony of the Beloved Disciple* (Grand Rapids: Baker, 2007).

saying is not regarded by John as an insult to Thomas. Rather, it is a promise to the readers who do not see but have John's account that was written quite specifically to help them to faith.

A final passing remark on the story of Thomas is necessary. Thomas is often referred to as "doubting Thomas." That is a fair description, however sympathetic we may be to his doubts. The account of Thomas shows that the writer of John's Gospel was aware that people in his day, as in ours, did not find the idea of Jesus and his resurrection something they could easily swallow. They needed evidence. John told the story of Jesus with that in mind.[7]

A major theme in the Gospel of John is that of witness. The assumption is that you would not believe in someone like Jesus without reason or evidence. There is considerable discussion within the narrative about witnesses. The author presents the Old Testament as a witness to Jesus. His miracles are seen as witnessing to his divine authority. His disciples are told that they are and will be witnesses to Jesus (John 5:30–47 and 15:26–27). They are sent out by Jesus in order to witness, with the help of the Holy Spirit.

John sees his account as part of that witness. The Gospel of John is ascribed to one of the disciples of Jesus who is given the mysterious title "the beloved disciple." In John 21:24 it is said specifically: "This is the disciple who

7. It is not the case that the story of Thomas encourages faith without sight of Jesus, as some argue. Rather, it encourages faith without physical sight of Jesus and on the basis of reliable testimony.

is bearing witness about these things and who has written these things, and we know that his testimony (witness) is true." Scholars debate whether the beloved disciple should be identified with John the son of Zebedee, as the early church believed. Further, who are the "we" of "we know that his testimony is true"? From our point of view, it is not necessary to answer those questions definitively. Whoever penned these words, they provide early evidence that the Gospel of John was seen to be an apostolic witness to Jesus to help people believe in him.

The picture is consistent in Matthew, Mark, Luke, and John. In their distinctive ways, the different accounts see the story and sayings of Jesus as the heart of the Christian good news and present the disciples of Jesus as having the particular role of passing his good news on to others. Further, the authors seem to understand themselves as continuing the work of the disciples, with their accounts of Jesus being versions of the good news that was being proclaimed across the Roman world and elsewhere. These written accounts are themselves important witnesses, since at the very least they are an outcome or end product of the oral tradition. The canonical gospels are primary evidence for the oral traditions that preceded them.

Of course, the writers' claims for themselves could be—and have been—questioned. It might be argued that they are all with one voice reading back the later outlook and practice of the Christian church (which did entail systematic teaching of the story of Jesus). They could be giving a rationale for their own writings, a radical departure from the earliest days of the church with its haphazard preservation of the traditions of Jesus. However, such skepticism is unjustified. All the evidence points in the same direction.[8] The first Christians told the story of Jesus, in order to bring people to faith, baptism, and faithful discipleship.

---

8. I have not included the apocryphal gospels in my discussion, despite the recent popular interest in them and the scholars who have argued for their value. In my opinion, they have a tenuous claim to antiquity and historicity. John P. Meier puts it more extremely, when he speaks of "a field of rubble, largely produced by the pious and wild imaginations of certain second-century Christians" in *The Roots of the Problem and the Person*, vol. 1 of *A Marginal Jew: Rethinking the Historical Jesus* (New York, Doubleday, 1991), 115.

CHAPTER 4

The Evidence of Paul

Paul's letters are the earliest extant Christian documents, dating from the end of the 40s CE.[1] Paul speaks of "receiving" traditions of Jesus (probably at the time when he became a believer in Jesus) and of "passing them on" when he took the good news out to the Mediterranean world (1 Cor 11:23; 15:1–2).[2] He thus attests to the existence and importance of oral tradition in the church; he also gives us many clues about the content of that tradition.[3]

1. There is a lot of interesting and important evidence of Jesus tradition in other New Testament letters, notably in 1 Peter and James. I focus on Paul because his letters are the most datable of the New Testament documents, and some of them at least are almost universally accepted as authentic by scholars—with good reason.

2. It is regularly observed that the verbs "received" and "'passed on" are "virtually technical terms in Jewish culture for the transmission of important traditions. . . . Hellenistic philosophies used these terms in transmitting their standard doctrines." See Anthony C. Thiselton, *The First Epistle to the Corinthians: A Commentary on the Greek Text*, NIGTC (Grand Rapids: Eerdmans, 2000), 867.

3. His evidence is the more striking in that it comes out incidentally

The claim that Paul was interested in, and well-informed about, the story of Jesus is not surprising given the interest of Luke. However, this point has not been accepted by all scholars. Some have argued the opposite, noting that Paul in his letters does not explicitly refer to Jesus's teaching with frequency. This stands in contrast to his regular and explicit use of the Old Testament.[4]

This "minimalist" view of Paul's use of Jesus tradition has been challenged by various scholars.[5] For example, Ulrich Luz affirms that "Paul must have told his converts something about the life of his risen Lord, whose incarnation, death, and resurrection he was proclaiming. Otherwise, his proclamation ("kerygma") would have been empty and inapplicable."[6] Luz is right in that conclusion, even if his word "something" is cautious.

---

when he is addressing church matters, not questions of Jesus and history (with the possible exception of 1 Cor 15).

4. Various Pauline texts have been misused to demonstrate his lack of interest in the historical Jesus. For example, in 2 Cor 5:16, Paul says "If indeed we once knew Christ according to flesh, now we do not." However, this text does not indicate Paul's lack of interest in the history of Jesus. Rather, he here affirms that, although he once had an unbeliever's view of Jesus, he now has a believer's view. In Gal 1:12, he says of his gospel: "I did not receive it from man, nor was I taught it, but it came through a revelation of Jesus Christ." He seems to be referring to his personal meeting with Jesus on the Damascus Road as a decisive moment. This meeting serves as a definitive proof against his critics who saw him as a second-hand apostle or evangelist who had not met or been commissioned by Jesus. But the implication is not that he got all his information about Jesus in that way. Some of it was "received" via human agents in the same way as he "passed it on."

5. Ulrich Luz, "The Use of Jesus-Traditions in the Pauline and Post-Pauline Letters," in *Exegetische Aufsätze*, WUNT 357 (Tübingen: Mohr Siebeck, 2016), 75–91.

6. Luz, "The Use of Jesus-Traditions in the Pauline and Post-Pauline Letters," 86.

In what follows, we will look first at some of the most important and widely accepted evidence for Paul's use of the oral traditions of and about Jesus. In a number of cases, Paul gives at least a hint that he is using such traditions.

1 Corinthians 15:1–3, which we have already noted, is particularly important and unambiguous evidence that Paul was interested in the traditions of Jesus. Further, this text proves that he told people about Jesus's life and teaching when establishing churches. He did not just offer them a wonderful mystical experience such as he had on the way to Damascus: "You can have one too!" Rather he puts it this way: "I want you to know, brothers, the gospel which I proclaimed to you . . . I passed on to you as of first importance what I also received that Christ died for our sins in accordance with the Scriptures, and that he was buried, and that he was raised on the third day in accordance with the Scriptures." This is nothing like the whole story of Jesus or his passion and resurrection; he is briefly summarizing what he said and reminding the Corinthians of it.[7] Paul does, however, go on from that pithy summary to list various witnesses who saw the risen Jesus. It is unlikely that when Paul proclaimed the good news he just gave his hearers a summary of key events lasting for half a

7. Scholars speak of it as a kerygmatic saying, as though that is necessarily different from telling the story. But *kērygma* is simply the Greek word for proclamation. What was proclaimed by Paul was undoubtedly more than a few pithy statements in 1 Cor 15:1–3, which are a kerygmatic summary.

minute! He will have told them much more, including about the witnesses to the resurrection whom he notes. He very probably told some of their stories of meeting the risen Jesus, in addition to his first-hand experience.[8] The two other people he names, Peter and James, were known to Paul. It is likely that he knew others among the more than five hundred people whom he refers to and who witnessed the resurrection.

1 Corinthians 11:23–26 provides compelling evidence that Paul told the stories and did not just provide some basic headlines. In context, he is lamenting the disastrous way that the Corinthians were meeting for the Lord's Supper. The rich Christians were living it up with eating and drinking. The poor Christians were getting very little. Paul is scathing about this. In the course of discussing their behavior, he says:

> I received from the Lord what I also passed on to you, that the Lord Jesus on the night that he was betrayed took bread, and when giving thanks he broke it and said "This is my body which is for

---

8. That story features very large in Paul's trial speeches in Acts, and also in Galatians (cf. Gal 1:13–24). His telling of his own story in all of those contexts makes sense, since he is defending himself and the validity of his gospel by explaining that he had a revelation of the risen Jesus. It was not the first time the story had been told to the Galatians, as is clear from his comment in 1:13 "You have heard of my former life." It is highly unlikely that his evangelism focused on his own story rather than on that of Jesus; the opposite is much more likely, i.e., that Paul told them the story and stories of Jesus when he proclaimed to them and when they became Christians. 1 Corinthians 15:1–3 is entirely credible: the stories of Jesus were the center of the good news that Paul brought to places like Corinth.

you. Do this in remembrance of me." In the same
way also the cup after supper, saying "This cup is
the new covenant in my blood. Do this, as often
as you drink it in remembrance of me." For as
often as you eat this bread and drink this cup,
you are proclaiming the Lord's death, until he
comes.[9]

The notable thing about this is that Paul specifically
speaks, once again, of having passed on traditions of Jesus to the Corinthian Christians. In this case, it is not a
summary like 1 Cor 15:1–3 on the resurrection; it is one
particular story of one particular event just before Jesus's
arrest and crucifixion, including words of Jesus.[10]

However, scholars do not agree that this passage

9. Paul's version of the Last Supper has striking resemblances to the
Lukan narrative (cf. Luke 22:7–23). Luke differs from Mark and Matthew
in various ways, agreeing with Paul in the wording "This cup is the new
covenant in my blood" and in the exhortation "Do this in remembrance
of me." The Paul-Luke links could be explained in terms of Paul's influence
on his companion Luke. But the distinctiveness of Luke's account is not
all explicable from Paul's account; Luke's reference to two cups of wine,
for example, is not paralleled in Paul. Luke's resurrection account also has
links to Paul, notably in the reference to the risen Jesus appearing first to
Peter (Luke 24:34; 1 Cor 15:5).

10. Jens Schröter, "Jesus and the Canon," in *Performing the Gospel:
Orality, Memory, and Mark*, ed. Richard A. Horsley, Jonathan A. Draper, and
John Miles Foley (Minneapolis: Fortress, 2006), 109, says of 1 Cor 11:23–25
that it is "quite obvious that he is referring not to words of the earthly
Jesus but to a Christian tradition and is thus placing it within a traditional
context." The opposite conclusion is more obvious: the tradition that was
passed on was very specifically a tradition about the earthly Jesus and
what he did and said. Yes, Paul speaks of "the Lord" and thinks of Jesus
as a present Lord and God. For Paul, Jesus was Lord during his ministry as
well as after the resurrection.

demonstrates that Paul passed on a significant portion of the story of Jesus. They identify 1 Cor 11:23–26 as a "liturgical tradition." That is plausible enough. This story had quite possibly become part of what the Christians said in their regular worship. However, the way Paul expresses himself is not in terms of reminding them of words said each Sunday in the Eucharist. It is in terms of the story of the supper that he passed on to them. The language ("on the night he was betrayed") suggests that the Corinthian Christians knew the story of the arrest of Jesus. It further suggests that the story of the passion was "passed on" by Paul and others.

This was not just in Corinth. In his letter to the Galatians, Paul laments that the Galatian Christians were being lured away from the "good news" as they heard it from Paul. He comments, "It was before your eyes that Jesus Christ was publicly portrayed as crucified" (Gal 3:1). The language is unusual, but Paul is not talking about a visual aid. Rather, he is referring to the description of the crucifixion that they had received when they became Christians. Paul's description went beyond the statement that "Christ died for our sins." The Galatians probably knew about the beatings and the nails that "marked" Jesus (hence Paul's enigmatic reference to the "marks'" of Jesus in Gal 6:17).

Earlier in Galatians there is another possible echo of the passion story. Paul speaks in Gal 4:4 of Jesus as sent into the world "born of a woman." This leads him directly into a comment about Christians sharing by adoption in Jesus's sonship and about God sending "the Spirit of his

Son into our hearts, crying 'Abba,' Father" (4:6). The very striking appearance of the Aramaic word "Abba" in the Greek letter of Galatians is best explained as an echo of Jesus's usage; this makes sense in the context since it is, Paul says, "the Spirit *of his Son*" who inspires the believer in this way. The use of "Abba" is directly attested in the gospels only within Mark's account of Jesus in Gethsemane (Mark 14:36). The fact that Mark records it here may be because the word was particularly associated with this part of the story of Jesus's passion and of the events leading up to Jesus's arrest ("handing over").[11] If that is the case, this is further evidence of Paul's knowledge of the passion narrative.[12] Even if it is not, the use of "Abba" affirms the strong influence of a Jesus tradition on Paul and the Pauline churches.

It is not surprising that Christians told the story of the crucifixion of Jesus when explaining the good news. It was at the very heart of their message. It needed explanation. It is hard, if not impossible, to imagine people

11. The use of the word "cry" in Gal 4:6 may be significant because the canonical gospels describe an intensely stressful experience in Gethsemane. Hebrews 5:7 refers to Jesus praying with loud "cries" and tears to the one who was able to save him from death, language that has often been linked to the Gethsemane story. See also Heb 13:12 for another possible indication of knowledge of the passion story in Hebrews. On Paul and Gethsemane, and more generally on Paul and the passion, see Dale Allison, *Constructing Jesus: Memory, Imagination, and History* (Grand Rapids: Baker), 387–433, especially 417–18. He thinks that Paul's verb "to be crucified with" (*sustauroō*) may reflect knowledge of Jesus being crucified with two other convicts.

12. There are various possible links between Paul's comments on prayer, especially in Rom 8, and the Gethsemane story, including the other Pauline use of "Abba" in Rom 8:15. See Wenham, *Paul*, 275–80.

not asking why Jesus, whom they were being invited to believe in, had been crucified. The evidence in Paul's letters affirms that the first Christians told the story both of his death and resurrection in relationship to the Old Testament Scriptures. The prominence of the story of the passion in all the canonical gospels suggests that describing, and to some extent explaining, the crucifixion was extremely important.[13]

Scholars have quite often recognized that the passion is one of the oldest parts of the story of Jesus to have been formulated by the early church. That view in itself leaves open the question of when that formulation took place. However, there is a good case for affirming that the first Christians must have told the story of the Lord's death shortly after his death. Paul speaks of "having received" the traditions of the Lord's Supper and of the resurrection. It is not unreasonable to infer that he "received them" at the very beginning of his Christian career, when he was converted (probably in the early 30s CE)—not by direct revelation from the risen Jesus—but from those who were already believers and who had already been persuading others.

---

13. Luz, "The Use of Jesus-Traditions in the Pauline and Post-Pauline Letters," 85, argues that the readers of 1 Corinthians would have known the passion story, including stories about Judas and the resurrection appearances. He comments, "Naturally, the kerygmatic significance of these events is most important for Paul, but this importance is based on a concrete story." Note also 1 Thess 2:15 and its reference to the role of Jewish people in the death of Jesus. See also the naming of Pilate in 1 Tim 6:13. Although 1 Timothy is widely regarded as late, the association of Pilate with the death of Jesus will have been widely known; compare Tacitus, *Ann.* 15.4.

In addition, it seems very unlikely that the first Christians started with Jesus's passion when they told the story of Jesus. To put the matter simply: when wanting to persuade people to believe in Jesus, they were unlikely to have said: "Well, let me tell you the story of how he was arrested and crucified." Despite the importance of the events around Jesus's death, you would not start with a crucifixion narrative in telling others the good news of Jesus.

The account of the Last Supper in Paul begins with "on the night that he was betrayed," and, as noted above, hints that Paul is not just relaying "a liturgical tradition." Rather, there was a known narrative, including what led up to the meal. The language itself begs the question: What led up to that night? And, so far as the passion narrative as a whole is concerned, the obvious question to ask will have been: Who was this person who had evoked devotion and hatred in almost equal quantities? And why should we believe in him? Just because he rose again? They would have wanted to know what had happened before his death.

At first sight Paul's evidence may seem to let us down on this. He does not refer to "passing on" pre-passion stories of Jesus's life and ministry, and some would say that he is conspicuously uninterested in that history. But that is not the case. Yes, the evidence for his use of Jesus traditions is especially clear with the last supper and resurrection, since the Corinthian Christians had serious problems relating to those narratives. But there is important evidence of his interest in Jesus's pre-passion teaching and ministry.

1 Corinthians 7:10–11 is one of the widely recognized references to Jesus's teaching. Paul is responding to the idea of some Corinthians that "a man should not touch a woman." He counters their suggestion that those Christians who are married should separate and have no sexual relations (no "touching" in that sense). In that context, Paul brings in Jesus's teaching against divorce. He quite specifically introduces what he says with "I give this charge, not I, but the Lord."[14] Paul then paraphrases the Lord's teaching on divorce in a way that has notable similarities to Jesus's two sayings as found in Mark 10:9–12. Jesus in Mark says "What God has joined together, let no one separate." He also clarifies by saying, "Whoever divorces his wife and marries another commits adultery." Paul also has a general statement "the wife should not separate from her husband," which is clarified "but if she does separate, let her remain unmarried."[15] It is entirely

14. After referring to the Lord's teaching, Paul reverts to his own teaching in 7:8: "But to the rest I say not the Lord." Schröter, "Jesus and the Canon," 104–22, argues that there was no interest in distinguishing genuine words of Jesus from other things, or even of preserving those words; rather there was "a free and living tradition, and therefore the idea of a fixed, authoritative form of that tradition must be abandoned" (110). But the clear impression is that Paul is distinguishing teaching of the Lord, albeit paraphrased, from other spiritual wisdom, including his own. Schröter speaks of a sphere of tradition, including sayings of Jesus but also other ingredients, e.g., from Jewish-Hellenistic ethics.

15. Luz, "The Use of Jesus-Traditions in the Pauline and Post-Pauline Letters," 86: "In the use of the verb *chorizō* (separate) it comes close to Mark 10:9 par.; in the form of a double prohibition it resembles Mark 10,11f par." Paul paraphrases the saying of Jesus and addresses it first to the wife, probably because of the Corinthian context. Margaret Y. MacDonald, "Women Holy in Body and Spirit in the Social Setting of 1 Corinthians 7," *NTS* 36 (1990): 161–81, esp. 170–71; David Wenham, "Paul's Use of the Jesus Tradition: Three Samples," in *The Jesus Tradition*

possible that he knew not just the sayings, but the whole story about Jesus responding to his questions about the legitimacy of divorce. This is strong evidence of Paul's knowledge about the teaching of Jesus and of its importance for him.

In 1 Cor 9 Paul speaks of his willingness to forgo his rights as an apostle. In that context, he discusses the rights and privileges of apostles, including their right to have food and drink provided. In the course of the discussion he comments that "the Lord commanded, that those who proclaim the gospel should get their living by the gospel." Nearly all scholars agree that Paul is referring to Jesus's teaching, as found in the mission discourses in Matthew and Luke. Jesus speaks of his apostles accepting food and drink provided for them: "The laborer is worthy of his hire" (Luke 10:7; cf. "his food" in Matt 10:11). Paul knows the teaching of Jesus and creatively applies it to his own apostleship.[16]

Scholars often accept that this verse and the saying

Outside the Gospels, ed. David Wenham, vol. 5 of *Gospel Perspectives* (Sheffield: JSOT, 1985), 7–15.

16. The saying is quoted directly in 1 Tim 5:18; but the dating and authorship of 1 Timothy is debated. Intriguingly, in 1 Cor 9, Paul is explaining why he has not been doing what Jesus said to the apostles, and some scholars have seen this as showing Paul's lack of respect for Jesus's teaching. If that were the case, it would still show that Jesus's teaching was known and seen as important in the church, so that Paul has to defend himself. His explanation is that he has not made use of a "right" given by Jesus for evangelistic reasons, themselves plausibly seen as deriving from Jesus (compare 1 Cor 9:19 with Mark 10:43–45 and perhaps 1 Cor 9:18 with Matt 10:8, and see further discussion below). Paul's use of his traditions is creative and flexible here and elsewhere, e.g., with the divorce saying being related to the question of celibacy.

about divorce are evidence of individual sayings of Jesus being known in the church. However, they rarely see them as indicating that the teaching of Jesus was learned and passed on in a systematic way, let alone as imagining that the pre-passion story of Jesus was passed on.

There is a good case for saying that it was not just a few isolated sayings that were passed on. Thus a comparison of 1 Cor 9 with Luke 9–10 suggests that Paul may well have had a version of the mission discourse(s) of Jesus in mind, not just one saying without any context. In both 1 Cor 9 and the Lukan passages, the focus is on apostles and "apostleship," there is reference to privileged eating and drinking, and there is the saying about the laborer.[17] It is at least feasible that Paul was familiar with some or all of the discourse, and indeed its context.[18]

In 1 Thess 5:2, Paul speaks about the Lord coming like a "thief in the night." This is a probable echo of Jesus's parabolic saying about the coming of the Son of Man, found in both Matthew and Luke (Matt 24:43, Luke 12:39). Paul says to the Thessalonians that "*you know accurately that* the day of the Lord will come like a thief" (5:2). This is a possible "tradition indicator."[19] In other

---

17. See recently Boyoung Kang, *Heralds and Community: An Enquiry into Paul's Conception of Mission and Its Indebtedness to the Jesus-Tradition* (Carlisle: Langham, 2016), 226–53. Biörn Fjärstedt, *Synoptic Tradition in 1 Corinthians: Themes and Clusters of Theme Words in 1 Corinthians 1–4 and 9* (Thesis, Uppsala, 1974), may go too far in identifying parallels, but the overall direction of his argument is persuasive.

18. The idea of some of such sayings "floating" around without any context is more assumed than argued. As argued here, memorable sayings of Jesus presumably had original contexts.

19. See Michael B. Thompson, *Clothed with Christ: The Example and*

words, Paul may here hint at a tradition that had been passed on to the Thessalonians. In this case Paul can say "you know accurately that" (ESV: "you are fully aware"), because he knows that they had been taught about Jesus, as well as his future coming and teaching. Near the beginning of the letter, Paul refers to how they turned to God from idols "to serve the living and true God and to wait for his Son from heaven" (1:9–10). They had been taught about the Lord's return, and knew the Lord's own parable. Further, it is probable that they learned about the thief-like coming through Jesus's teaching. It is improbable that anyone in the Christian church would have come up with the comparison of Jesus to a thief, whereas Jesus—the great teller of parables—could perfectly well have used the analogy to emphasize the unexpectedness of his coming. Paul is notably circumspect in speaking not of "the Lord's coming," but of "*the day of* the Lord" coming like a thief.[20]

One wonders whether it was just the one short parable that Paul knew, or whether he knew it in the context of other teachings of the Lord about the parousia. In the

---

Teaching of Jesus in Romans 12:1–15:13 (Sheffield: JSOT, 1991), 28–36, for useful discussion of various possible tradition indicators found in Paul.

20. Some scholars have wanted to turn the argument on its head and to say that Paul's teaching about the Lord's coming was the source of the thief comparison, and that the tradition in the canonical gospels got it from Paul not Paul from Jesus. This is not plausible, since (1) Paul would hardly have compared Jesus to a thief; (2) the idea is well-attested in the New Testament, being found in 2 Peter and Rev 3:3; 16:15. It could all have started in Paul, but it is more plausible that it started with Jesus; (3) Paul acknowledges that he is drawing in some sense on "the word of the Lord" in this section of 1 Thessalonians (see 4:15).

preceding verses in 1 Thessalonians, Paul refers to the Lord coming from heaven "with a cry of command, with the voice of an archangel, and with the trumpet of God," and meeting with his people, living and departed (4:13–18). The passage is strongly reminiscent of the portrayal of Jesus's coming on the clouds with his angels to gather his elect in Matt 24:29–31, Mark 13:24–27, and Luke 21:25–28.

It is not possible to prove that Paul has Jesus's teaching in mind in this paralleled material. However, it is intriguing that he prefaces his description with "This we declare to you by the word of the Lord" (4:15). Is this another "tradition indicator"? If so, it would indicate that he is drawing on a tradition of Jesus's teaching for this material and not just for the parable of the thief. Scholars have doubted this, not least because Paul in his "declaration" is addressing the worries of the Thessalonian Christians about believers who have died—"fallen asleep" as he puts it—before the Lord's return. Scholars have struggled to find any word of Jesus that addresses that question. As a result, they wonder whether he is referring to unknown sayings of Jesus, a prophetic word of the Lord, or his own authoritative teaching. What has been missed by scholars is that Jesus's parable of the wise and foolish virgins in Matt 25:1–13, which comes shortly after the thief parable in Matthew, could have been what Paul had in mind. This parable specifically pictures girls who fall "asleep" and then the "rising up" of wise girls "to meet" with the bridegroom and to be "with him" in the feast. Similar language is used when Paul discusses Christians who are "falling asleep" (i.e., dying), "rising up," and then going "to meet" and be "with the Lord." [21] It makes sense that Paul was applying the parable about the delay of the Lord's coming and the arrival of the kingdom of God to their anxieties about departed loved ones.[22] Many scholars fail even to note this possible connection.[23] There is a real possibility that much of Paul's teaching on the parousia in chapters 4 and 5 is based on traditions of Jesus's own teaching. The strong evidence in connection with the saying about the thief and Paul's specific reference to "the word of the Lord" point us in that direction.[24]

21. The same distinctive phrase "to meet" (*eis apantēsin* in the Greek) is used by Paul and Matthew.

22. Despite Michael W. Pahl, *Discerning the "Word of the Lord": The "Word of the Lord" in 1 Thessalonians 4:15* (London: T&T Clark, 2009), 18, who acknowledges Jesus traditions in 1 Thessalonians but does not recognize the parable of the virgins. He claims, unpersuasively, that there is a "relative lack of significant and verbal agreement between that parable and 1 Thess. 4:16–17a."

23. Many scholars view the parable of the thief as Q material and, therefore, part of the early tradition, whereas the parable of the virgins is only in Matthew, as is the trumpet of Matt 24:31 in the description of the Son of Man's coming. Such M material tends to be seen by scholars as relatively late and unreliable. But Paul is drawing on oral tradition, and there is every possibility that it included other traditions as well as the parable of the thief. Intriguingly, Luke 12:35 preserves a saying about keeping lamps burning. It is possible that he knew the Matthean parable. So was the parable of the virgins perhaps also in Q? See further David Wenham, "Critical Blindness, Wise Virgins, and the Law of Christ: Three Surprising Examples of Jesus Tradition in Paul," in *The Message of Jesus: John Dominic Crossan and Ben Witherington III in Dialogue*, ed. Robert B. Stewart (Augsburg: Fortress, 2013), 183–203.

24. Jens Schröter, *From Jesus to the New Testament: Early Christian Theology and the Jesus Traditions* (Tübingen: Mohr Siebeck; Waco: Baylor, 2013), discusses 1 Thess 4:15–19. Yet, he fails to note the possible echoes of the parable of the virgins and the close proximity of these verses to the thief saying. He is equally cursory in his comment on 1 Cor 9:14, not noting how the context is Paul discussing his apostleship (including his equality

We have seen that Paul probably knew ethical traditions of Jesus (at least the one saying about divorce), some of Jesus's instructions to his apostles (at least the one saying about the laborer being worthy of his hire), and eschatological traditions (at least the saying about the thief). In each case, he takes the tradition as authoritative, even when he interprets it loosely.

It is very probable that Paul knew other traditions as well. His letter to the Romans includes a string of possible allusions to traditions from Jesus.[25] In Rom 12:14–19, Paul writes the following on non-retaliation: "Bless those who persecute you, bless and do not curse . . . do not repay anyone evil for evil." This language is highly reminiscent of Jesus's words in the Sermon on the Mount (Matt 5:43–45) and Sermon on the Plain (Luke 6:27–28) concerning love of enemies.[26]

The priority of love is emphasized throughout Rom 12–13, as well as elsewhere in Paul's letters (most famously in 1 Cor 13). This parallels Jesus's similar emphasis. Paul's particular explanation in Rom 13:8–10 that "the one who loves his neighbor has fulfilled the Law" and "love is the fulfilling of the Law" is reminiscent of Matt 22:34–40 and Mark 12:28–34, with the Matthew passage including the words, "On these two commandments hang all the Law and the Prophets." The idea of love ful-

---

to other apostles), and even on 1 Cor 11:23b–25 asserting with surprising confidence that it "cannot be traced back—at least in this form—to the earthly Jesus," 78–82.

25. See Thompson, *Clothed in Christ*, on Rom 12–15.

26. See also 1 Cor 4:12.

filling the Law also has a parallel in Matt 5, where Jesus's saying about having come "to fulfill all the Law and the Prophets" (v. 17) is followed by the so-called antitheses (vv. 20–48), where Old Testament and traditional Jewish teaching is contrasted with Jesus's ethical values—"but I say to you," climaxing in the command to love, even your enemy.[27]

Another possible and potentially very significant echo of Jesus's teaching is Rom 14:14: "I know and am persuaded *in the Lord Jesus* that nothing is unclean in itself." The phrase "in the Lord Jesus" is a possible hint that Paul is recalling teaching of Jesus as attested, for example, in Mark 7:16–19 where Jesus says, "there is nothing coming from outside a person that can defile a person, because it does not go into his heart, but into his stomach and goes out into the drain, thus cleansing all foods." The context in Mark is the response of Jesus to questions about the ritual washing of hands and other things. However, the Markan "cleansing all foods" looks like Mark applying the teaching of Jesus about external and internal cleanliness to the different question of clean and unclean foods, similar to Paul in Rom 14.[28] Paul and Mark may plausibly be seen as understanding the Jesus tradition in the same way in order to address a question that was extremely important as the Jewish church moved into Gentile mission.[29]

---

27. See Luz, "The Use of Jesus-Traditions in the Pauline and Post-Pauline Letters," 84.

28. See Joel Marcus, *Mark 1–8: A New Translation*, AB 27 (New York: Doubleday, 1999), 452–55.

29. See Mark 7:3–4.

The possibility that this tradition of Jesus was known to Paul and also to his readers may be confirmed by the evidence of 1 Cor 6:12–13, where Paul is responding to some of the men in the Corinthian church who are going to prostitutes, and apparently justifying their actions by saying that "all things are permissible," i.e., by an appeal to Christian freedom, and by saying "foods are for the stomach and the stomach for foods and God will destroy (or nullify) both one and the other." [30] This second statement about foods and the stomach could simply reflect their neo-Platonic ideas of the body as a temporary shell, but they could also have been influenced by Christian traditions both on the subject of freedom and also on what defiles the body. If Jesus said in relation to physical cleanness and uncleanness that nothing from outside the body defiles the person—using the example of food (that passes through the stomach and then goes out)—that could logically be applied also to sexual intercourse. That logic makes sense of the reference in 1 Cor 6:13 to food and stomach; both words are present in the Markan tradition.[31]

30. The possible connection is explored in Wenham, *Paul*, 92–97; see also Hanna Stettler, *Heiligung bei Paulus: Ein Beitrag aus biblisch-theologischer Sicht*, WUNT 2.368 (Tübingen: Mohr Siebeck, 2014), 329.

31. Mark's "cleansing all foods" is probably an attempt to resolve the contentious issue of Gentile converts and Jewish dietary rules, although it might also be that Mark specifically relates Jesus's words to "foods" in order to exclude any idea that they might also cover sex! Matthew is often thought to have eliminated the Markan "cleansing all foods" because he is on the conservative Jewish-Christian side of the early Christian argument on the question of clean and unclean food (Matt 15:17–20). However, it is possible that Matthew is working with a tradition of Jesus's words that did not have the Markan phrase at all (so James D. G. Dunn, *Jesus, Paul, and*

Another plausible connection between Paul and Jesus exists in Gal 6:2 where Paul writes, "Bear one another's burdens and so fulfill the law of Christ." The phrase "the law of Christ" has puzzled scholars. Some speculate that it is a "tradition indicator." They hold that Paul has in mind the "love your neighbor as yourself" command, as endorsed by Jesus in his teaching. However, that command was from the Law of Moses, not a distinctive teaching of Jesus. Others have suggested that the reference is not to a particular teaching of Jesus, but to his self-giving lifestyle. This solution is attractive, even if the choice of the word "law" is not obvious in that case. However, a preferable and more comprehensive explanation is that Paul has in mind Jesus's instruction to his disciples to have a different lifestyle from other leaders, as in Mark 10:43–45, "It is not so among you, but whoever wishes to be great among you shall be your servant, and whoever wishes to be first among you, shall be slave of all. For the Son of Man also came not to be served but to serve and give his life a ransom for many." In support of this connection, the tradition of Jesus calling his disciples to a life of serving is attested in the canonical gospels, coming not just in Mark 10 and the parallel passage in Matt 20, but also in Mark 9:35, Matt 23:11, Luke 22:24–27, and John 13:4–17. Further, in nearly every case, this lifestyle is identified by Jesus as

---

the Law [Westminster: John Knox, 1990], 40–44) and that he achieves the clarification—that it applies to foods (and not sex!)—by modifying Jesus's saying so that Jesus refers specifically to "whatever enters the mouth" not defiling a person.

something that is to be distinctive of his followers; so "the law of Christ" is apt (Mark 10:42–43; Matt 20:25–26; 23:8–11; Luke 22:25–26; John 13:35). In addition, the call to such living is regularly and specifically linked to Jesus's own lifestyle and example (esp. the cross). It is thus "the law of Christ," in that he lived by it, and it is to be imitated by Jesus's followers. This is something emphasized by Paul most strikingly in Phil 2:5–11.[32] Also in support of this connection, Paul elsewhere has what can plausibly be seen as echoes of this teaching of the Lord, which Jesus himself also modeled. For example, in 1 Cor 9:19, Paul says, "Though being free from all I have made myself a slave to all, that I might win the more." His language sounds very similar to that in Mark 10: "Whoever would be first among you will be slave of all . . . for the Son of Man came . . . to be served and to give his life a ransom for many." Note also Gal 5:13: "through love be slaves to one another." This comes shortly before 6:2 and is plausibly viewed as a definition of "the law of Christ" for Paul. Finally, the closest parallel to "the law of Christ" is Jesus's word in John 13:34–35: "A new commandment I give to you, that you love one another as I have loved you. By this all will know that you are my disciples if you have love for one another." This "new command" of Jesus comes after his outstanding act of slave-like service in washing the disciples' feet.

The evidence demonstrates that Paul knew and used a wide range of traditions about Jesus: stories and

32. Compare also 2 Cor 8:7–9.

sayings. A number of the examples have "tradition indicators." At times, Paul speaks explicitly of passing on a tradition. At other times, there is a more oblique reference, as with "I am persuaded in the Lord Jesus" or "the law of Christ."

Some of the examples, (e.g., the passion, resurrection, divorce, laborer, and thief) have been recognized by scholars who would argue that Paul was not very familiar or really very interested in Jesus traditions. What they fail to see is the cumulative weight of even the modest amount of evidence discussed so far and the importance of Dunn's argument about oral tradition as the default position.

Some scholars question: Why is there not much more explicit use of Jesus tradition?[33] In response to this Luz comments on his suspicion that "the genre of a text is one of the elements that can be decisive for the frequency and the way in which Jesus-traditions are used." He refers to "real letters where the author's dialogue with the recipients prevails and where a common tradition forms a common basis between author and his recipients, allowing them to recognize allusions and echoes

---

33. Scholars contrast the paucity of explicit references to the Jesus tradition with Paul's frequent use of the Old Testament, but Luz, "The Use of Jesus-Traditions in the Pauline and Post-Pauline Letters," 87, comments: "Paul's use of Jesus-traditions is not fundamentally different from his use of Scriptures: Many of them are explicit quotations with formal introductions, others—Hays calls them 'echoes'—are invisible, unmarked and a part of the Pauline text." See extensively on this Yongbom Lee, *Paul. Scribe of Old and New: Intertextual Insights for the Jesus-Paul Debate* (Edinburgh: T&T Clark, 2015).

to Jesus-traditions."[34] Luz is right in his suspicion and comment. Paul's letters are not gospels but are occasional letters written mainly to people whom he knows, addressing their specific issues (whether to do with the Lord's Supper, the resurrection, or questions of singleness or eschatology). In those contexts, he often refers them back to traditions, *which they had already been taught and knew already* and which he or his team had already passed on. Paul can and does presuppose knowledge. He often echoes traditions of Jesus without indicating that he is doing so.[35]

Luz's own modest conclusion is that Paul's readers had "general knowledge about the life of Jesus," but he comments, "About contents and details I do not want to speculate here." His caution is understandable, not least because of the brevity of his article. Although wild speculation is definitely to be avoided, the opposite danger is also to be avoided. If oral tradition is the default position and Paul used a substantial amount of Jesus tradition, scholars should look for significant parallels. It is a fact that there were substantial oral traditions of Jesus. It is

---

34. Luz, "The Use of Jesus-Traditions in the Pauline and Post-Pauline Letters," 82.

35. On the question of Paul's infrequent direct citation of Jesus traditions, see, among others, Rainer Riesner, "Paulus und die Jesus-Überlieferung," in *Evangelium Schriftauslegung Kirche. Festschrift für Peter Stuhlmacher zum 65. Geburtstag*, ed. Jostein Ådna, Scott J. Hafemann, and Otfried Hofius (Göttingen: Vandenhoeck & Ruprecht, 1997), 347–65. It has often been observed that it is not only Paul who does not constantly quote Jesus. There are not many quotations in Acts, although the author also wrote Luke's Gospel. There are not many in the Johannine letters, despite the Gospel of John.

also a fact that these traditions were known to Paul. Further, these traditions were passed on to the churches he founded, and, of course, many of them ended up in Matthew, Mark, Luke, and John.

Many scholars seem resistant to explaining things via oral tradition, seeking other explanations. For example, if Matthew is basing his eschatological discourse on Mark, then the parable of the virgins is added by Matthew and is often seen as a Matthean redactional creation. If John is the last of the canonical gospels (as most scholars maintain), then Paul is considered unlikely to be referring to the very Johannine "new commandment" of Jesus (compare 1 John 3–5). However, as soon as it is remembered that Paul and his traditions about Jesus predate every extant gospel and that all the evangelists would have had access to the oral tradition—not to mention the fact that they all claim to be recording Jesus traditions!—then the picture changes radically. The Pauline evidence deserves to be taken very seriously indeed.

There is, in fact, a strong case for identifying much more Jesus tradition in Paul.[36] For example, Luz himself hesitantly notes Paul's few references to "the kingdom of God."[37] It does not appear to have been Paul's favored

36. Significant recent work includes Maureen W. Yeung, *Faith in Jesus and Paul: A Comparison with Special Reference to "Faith That Can Remove Mountains" and "Your Faith Has Healed/Saved You"*, WUNT 2.147 (Tübingen: Mohr Siebeck, 2002); Gerry Schoberg, *Perspectives of Jesus in the Writings of Paul: A Historical Examination of Shared Core Commitments with a View to Determining the Extent of Paul's Dependence on Jesus* (Cambridge: James Clarke, 2014).

37. Luz, "The Use of Jesus-Traditions in the Pauline and Post-Pauline Letters," 83.

way of expressing the good news of Jesus. Yet, some of his references do sound suspiciously like echoes of Jesus, notably 1 Cor 6:9, "Don't you know that unrighteous people will not inherit the kingdom of God?" (compare Matt 5:20, "Unless your righteousness exceed that of the scribes and Pharisees you will not enter the kingdom of heaven," and Rom 14:17, "The kingdom of God is not a matter of eating and drinking, but of righteousness, peace and joy," and also 1 Cor 4:20).[38] Others have argued that Paul's emphasis on Jesus as the new Adam may be linked to the unanimous verdict of the canonical gospels that Jesus spoke of himself as "Son of Man."[39] There are numerous other possible echoes.[40] Even without exploring these here, we

38. Paul's emphasis on "righteousness" has often been contrasted with Matthew's emphasis on righteousness in his account of Jesus's teaching, but there is a case for a connection between them. See David Wenham, "The Rock on Which to Build: Some Mainly Pauline Observations about the Sermon on the Mount," in *Built Upon the Rock: Studies in the Gospel of Matthew*, ed. Daniel M. Gurtner and John Nolland (Grand Rapids: Eerdmans, 2007), 186–206. Luz, "The Use of Jesus-Traditions in the Pauline and Post-Pauline Letters," 78, goes in a very different and implausible direction when he accepts the view that 1 Pet 3:14 (with its obvious similarity to Matt 5:10) and 2:12 are not evidence of early oral tradition, but of "a secondary oralization of Jesus-traditions on the basis of the text of the First Gospel."

39. See most recently Yongbom Lee, *The Son of Man As the Last Adam* (Eugene, OR: Pickwick, 2012).

40. Wenham, *Paul*, remains the most comprehensive survey of the large amount of possible evidence, among other things examining evidence for Paul's knowledge of the transfiguration story, of the story of Mary and Martha, and the saying about moving mountains. Note also, Detlef Häusser, *Christusbekenntnis und Jesusüberlieferung bei Paulus*, WUNT 2.210 (Tübingen: Mohr Siebeck, 2006). Christine Jacobi, *Jesusüberliefering bei Paulus? Analogien zwischen den echten Paulusbriefen und den synoptischen Evangelien* (Berlin: Walter de Gruyter, 2015). She follows her mentor Jens Schröter in doubting whether there is evidence for a deliberate conserving of Jesus

may conclude that Paul is a very significant witness to the existence of a substantial and important oral tradition of words and actions of Jesus.

A final important argument about Paul and the Jesus tradition relates to the way he connects the idea of apostleship to the proclamation of the gospel and the story of Jesus. First, Paul's claim to apostleship is an important and sensitive one. It is sensitive because his opponents likely questioned him on this point on the grounds that he could not have the status of apostle, because he was not with Jesus (indeed he had been a vicious opponent!). This is suggested by the rather defensive or apologetic tone of Paul's references, notably in Gal 1–2, where his Judaizing opponents have been criticizing his gospel of Christian freedom and comparing him unfavorably with the undisputed apostles in Jerusalem. It is also in question at 1 Cor 9:1 ("Am I not an apostle?") and in 1 Cor 15:9, where he speaks of himself as the least of the apostles because of his personal history. Second, Paul accepts the view of his opponents that the qualification for apostleship is eyewitness experience of Jesus—and probably being "sent" by Jesus (the Greek verb being *apostellō*, "to send"). They question him on precisely that ground, since he was not a follower of Jesus or a witness of his resur-

---

traditions and in being skeptical about finding echoes and allusions in Paul's letters, even though some traditions have been absorbed into the traditions of the church. She finds me and others guilty of circular reasoning that presupposes its conclusions; I hope this book in a small way counters that view, although of course sound argument often involves some circularity with the thesis being proposed then being tested to see whether it accounts for the data and evidence.

rection when he was on earth. He accepts the premise about apostleship and eyewitness but asks them in 1 Cor 9:1: "Am I not an apostle? Have I not seen the Lord?" (both questions in Greek expect an affirmative answer). He is likely referring to his experience on the way to Damascus, as is evident from Gal 1, where he describes the experience and speaks of God "revealing his Son" to him (Gal 1:16). He knows that people could dispute whether that was an appearance comparable to that of the first apostles. In fact, he speaks in 1 Cor 15:8 of himself as an oddity—"one untimely born" (literally "as to an abortion," a much-discussed phrase). But however odd and controversial it may be, Paul is very clear that he qualifies as an eyewitness.[41]

Third, Paul very specifically connects his own apostleship with the gospel that he proclaimed. In Rom 1:1–5, Paul's summary of the good news arises out of his description of himself as "called to be an apostle." He is called to be an apostle "set apart for the good news" of God. His apostleship is all about bringing the good news of Jesus to the nations. In 1 Cor 15, Paul summarizes in "what terms I proclaimed to you the good news," narrates

---

41. Stan Porter, *When Paul Met Jesus: How An Idea Got Lost in History* (Cambridge: Cambridge University Press, 2016), attempts to show that Paul did meet Jesus in his lifetime. Although intriguing, his thesis is ultimately unpersuasive. Paul may well have been in Palestine at times during Jesus's ministry, but that does not mean that the young Pharisaic student will have met the Galilean false prophet, even when Jesus visited Jerusalem for festivals—when the city was massively overcrowded. Of course, if Porter's thesis were correct, it would mean that Paul had firsthand information about Jesus, not just what "he received" from other Christians.

the story of Jesus, focusing on his death and especially his resurrection, and concludes it with a discussion of his apostleship: "Whether it is I or they, so we proclaim and so you believe" (15:1, 11). Similarly, in Gal 1, the discussion is about his gospel and his apostleship, the two being very closely connected, as also in what follows (see Gal 2:7-8).

Fourth, Paul insists that his gospel is not different from the gospel proclaimed by the Jerusalem apostles. He emphasizes this clearly in Galatians where his opponents were saying that his gospel was seriously deficient, as well as that his apostleship was bogus. Paul insists that the gospel that he proclaimed was given him by revelation (1:12)[42]—there is no valid alternative gospel—and that in due course his gospel was recognized by "the pillars" of the church in Jerusalem (2:1–10). It was not recognized as an alternative but still acceptable gospel; Paul is emphatic that there is only one gospel, as proclaimed by himself or by Peter, the only difference being that his mission field was the Gentiles and that of the Jerusa-

---

42. One might infer from this that Paul's gospel was an account of his revelatory experience on the road to Damascus and nothing like the narratives in the canonical gospels. However, it is wholly improbable that his experience was all or even the core of what he proclaimed. It was a much bigger message than that, and Paul claims that it was the same gospel as was proclaimed by the Jerusalem apostles. His Damascus road experience was important and formative, but the implication is not that he received all his understanding of the gospel he proclaimed directly from heaven. He told the Galatians, among other things, the story of the cross (3:1) and Jesus's use of the term "Abba" (4:6). Paul probably mentioned the first apostles, the primacy of Peter (2:8; Peter too did not confer with flesh and blood, but had a revelation of the Son, Matt 16:16–20), Jesus's command to his followers to "be slaves to one another in love" (Gal 5:13), and even possibly Jesus's virgin birth (see ch. 7 below).

lem leaders was the circumcised. As he says in 1 Cor 15: "whether it was I or they, so we proclaim" (15:11). Fifth, the conclusion of these different observations must be that the gospel that "he" and "they" proclaimed is the story of Jesus as attested by the eyewitnesses and apostles. That is suggested by the mini-gospel narrative of 1 Cor 15:1–11 and by the summary of his gospel in Rom 1:3–4. The original apostles were obviously in a very strong position to tell the whole story as eyewitnesses, having been with Jesus during his ministry and "sent out" by Jesus. Paul was in a weaker position in that he was not there and he did, necessarily, "receive" traditions of Jesus from others. Yet, Paul insists that he had an equally valid eyewitness experience of the risen Lord and commissioning by the Lord as the other apostles and that he learned the essence of his gospel in that dramatic experience. So, although Paul is certainly vulnerable to people questioning his apostleship and the authority of his interpretation of Jesus, he is confident that he is a genuinely called apostle, sent out like those sent during Jesus's ministry. They proclaim the same message. In 1 Cor 9, he speaks of his apostleship and applies to himself Jesus's words about the laborer being worthy of his hire: "the Lord instructed that those who proclaim the gospel get their living by the gospel" (9:14). Paul, perhaps not surprisingly, takes the same view as Luke about the role of the apostle and about the gospel of Jesus, being the story of Jesus—his ministry, death, and resurrection.

What did the first Christians say about Jesus? Paul is an important witness who gives us every reason to believe that his good news—like the good news of the "original" apostles and leaders of the Jerusalem church—had a narrative of Jesus's life and ministry at its center. Echoes and allusions to that early oral tradition in his letters give us important glimpses into what the narrative contained.

CHAPTER 5

The Oral Tradition in the Gospels

Like an archaeologist who surveys the field to see whether things he has been told by others are supported by artifacts and other findings in the field, we will ask whether there are things in the canonical gospels that look like oral traditions or are best explained as such. Our conclusion will be strongly affirmative, i.e., recognition of a strong oral tradition unlocks features of the texts.

In the nineteenth and early twentieth centuries, notable scholars—e.g., B. F. Westcott—supported the idea that there was a strong "oral" tradition in the early church.[1] Scholars generally came to abandon that view, concluding that the similarities between the canonical gospels are best explained via literary dependence, with most eventually settling on the view that Matthew and Luke used Mark and another collection of Jesus-sayings, the famous Q source. Matthew and Luke were

1. B. F. Westcott, *Introduction to the Study of the Gospels* (London: Macmillan, 1895).

thought to have had some additional sources of their own, the M and L sources.[2] The triumph of this view made any idea of a strong pre-written gospel tradition as foundational to all the written gospels superfluous, or so it seemed.

The rise of form criticism helped kill off the idea of such a strong oral tradition, since form-critical analysis led many to the conclusion that they were composed of stories and sayings that had circulated in the church in the pre-literary period in a relatively haphazard way, being used in this or that context ("Sitz im Leben," to use the famous German phrase), without a connected narrative.[3] This common argument maintains that people eventually did start collecting the traditions (with the passion narrative being one of the first major collections). The author of Mark developed a new literary genre, the gospel.

The form critics did make some valid observations about the stories and sayings, noting how they have been shaped for the purpose of proclaiming and teaching, not just for historical or biographical interest; hence the lack of information about Jesus's appearance, early life, and the vagueness of much of the chronology in the canonical

2. The scholar in the English-speaking world who did most in making the two/four-document hypothesis popular was B. H. Streeter in his *The Four Gospels* (London: Macmillan, 1930). For two excellent surveys of synoptic research, see Mark Goodacre, *The Synoptic Problem: A Way through the Maze* (London: Sheffield Academic, 1996), and Bird, *The Gospel of the Lord*.

3. Cf. Rudolf Bultmann, *The History of the Synoptic Tradition*, trans. John Marsh (Oxford: Blackwell, 1963).

gospels. That observation in no way undermines the idea of a strong early oral gospel tradition. If one imagines the first apostles proclaiming and teaching about Jesus, they would, from the start, have focused on the religiously important aspects of Jesus, without including less significant items.[4]

Something that could be thought to support the form critics' view of a fluid and loose early gospel tradition is the variation among the narratives, including the different placing of various stories. For example, the calming of the storm in Matthew before Jesus's block of teaching in parables but after in Mark (Matt 8:23–27; Mark 4:35–41). Another example: in Luke, Jesus narrates the parable of the lost sheep when criticized for associating with sinners; in Matthew, Jesus is discussing problems within the church community (Luke 15:3–7; Matt 18:12–14). The force of these observations is not entirely clear. These phenomena may reflect the relative freedom of the evangelists to move their material around to suit their writing goals.[5]

That point about their editorial freedom is one of the major planks in the argument of form critics and later of some redaction critics who maintain that the writers

---

4. Although it is often noted that Mark's Gospel does have the odd incidental detail (e.g., the cushion in the boat, the greenness of the grass, etc.).

5. That comment is not meant to exclude the obvious possibility that a parable like that of the lost sheep (or any other piece of Jesus's teaching) might have been used more than once in different contexts by Jesus himself. For a forceful critique of the form-critical model, see Bauckham, *Jesus the Eyewitnesses*, ch. 21.

and their predecessors were not interested in preserving coherent tradition, but only in using traditions of Jesus for their own theological purposes.

However, that argument is false, for several reasons. (1) The writers of the canonical gospels had their own theological agendas. Luke probably did know Mark. Yet, his theological agenda, no less than Mark's agenda, was to tell the story of Jesus of Nazareth in a way that made clear his importance and relevance. He did not see himself as doing something new but largely went with Mark. He did not always follow Mark's order of events, because he believed that the story could be told more effectively—but no less reliably—by a different arrangement (for example, by introducing Jesus's ministry with the story of Jesus in the synagogue in Nazareth, Luke 4:16–30). Matthew too, if he knew Mark, reproduced the basic Markan story. Yet, he added to it and shaped it for his purposes. Both Matthew and Luke, if they used Mark, attest their belief in preserving traditions of Jesus, largely as they received them. (2) The picture that scholars have so often seemed to assume of how Matthew and Luke wrote their narrative, with Mark as their source, is quite unsatisfactory and improbable. The unspoken—perhaps unrecognized and unintended—assumption seems to be that, when Matthew used Mark, for example, he only had Mark's version of a particular story to draw on. This is entirely improbable. Should one imagine that when, for example, Matthew read the parables of Mark 4 (or the story of Jesus calming the storm, healing the Gerasene demoniac, or feeding the five thousand) that he had never heard any of these sayings and stories before he read them in Mark? It is a wholly unlikely scenario. Scholars often seem to operate as though Matthew had one source for much of the time, which he copied out sometimes word for word, sometimes making stylistic and theological changes that struck him. However, even on the most usual source theory (Matthew using Mark, Q, and special M material), it is entirely probable that Q or M material would have had some—perhaps many—of the Markan stories. Therefore, Matthew would have had more than one source when using Mark.[6] In any case, it is totally unlikely that Matthew discovered most of the stories and sayings when he read or heard Mark's Gospel. He will have known them, many of them at least, through the oral teaching of the church. Matthew, and Luke similarly, had more than one source for the stories.[7]

Scholars who accept the two-source hypothesis cheerfully endorse the idea of overlapping sources in instances of so-called Mark and Q overlap. These are passages where Matthew and Luke are following the line of Mark's story and quite probably using Mark. They both make the same striking changes or additions to Mark's account. Thus, for example, in the accounts of

---

6. Similarly with L for Luke.

7. The picture in any case of Matthew and Luke with a scroll of Mark simply copying it out is questionable. Werner Kelber comments that "texts used for the composition of another text . . . were often assimilated through hearing and 'interior dictation' rather than strict copying," *The Oral and the Written Gospel: The Hermeneutics of Speaking and Writing in the Synoptic Tradition, Mark, Paul, and Q* (Bloomington: Indiana University Press, 1997), xxii.

Jesus's baptism by John the Baptist, Matthew and Luke have the same basic story as Mark. In addition, they both have the saying of John: "Whose winnowing fork is in his hand, and he will clear his threshing floor and gather his wheat into the barn, but the chaff he will burn with unquenchable fire" (Matt 3:12 and Luke 3:17), which Mark does not have. In the account of Jesus being accused of casting out demons by the power of the devil, where Matthew and Luke are supposed to be following Mark (3:22–27), both Matthew and Luke have Jesus respond to his critics with words not found in Mark: "But if I by the Spirit or finger of God cast out demons, then the kingdom of God has come upon you" (Matt 12:28 and Luke 11:20).

These and many other examples strongly suggest that Matthew and Luke sometimes draw on a non-Markan source, even when they are following Mark. Their agreements "against Mark" point in that direction. Many scholars agree that the stories of Jesus's baptism and temptation were in Mark *and* in the Q source. Matthew and Luke have used both sources.

That explanation could be right: one would expect Mark's account of Jesus's ministry and the Q collection of Jesus's sayings to overlap. And yet, is there any need for the highly hypothetical Q, when the oral tradition was strong? The apparently persuasive reply from defenders of Q is that the agreements of Matthew and Luke in wording and order of contents are often too close to be explained in terms of oral tradition. However, this argument reflects our modern experience of memory being very fallible and inaccurate. It fails to take into account the evidence from non- or semi-literary cultures, ancient and modern, in which memorization can be accurate and extensive. Some proponents of Q have taken this on board and argued that Q itself could have been an oral tradition (or more than one tradition).[8] That view might be hardly distinguishable from the argument of this book, except that the evidence points to a much more extensive oral tradition than the traditionally conceived Q.

In addition to the major agreements of Matthew and Luke against Mark, which can be explained as Mark and Q overlaps, there are many so-called "minor agreements." An example is the saying, found shortly before the parable of the mustard seed, on the purpose of parables, where Mark has "to you the mystery of the kingdom of God has been given" (Mark 4:11) and Matthew and Luke have "to you is given to know the mysteries" (Matt 13:11 and Luke 8:10). Scholars tend not to ascribe this agreement of Matthew and Luke to Q, because it is in a section where they are following Mark and drawing on Mark, not another source.[9] Other examples are in narrative passages. For example, Mark 14:65 has the guards striking the blindfolded Jesus and saying "Prophesy"; Matt 26:68 and Luke 22:64 both add the question: "Who struck you?"

8. E.g., the notable Joachim Jeremias, *New Testament Theology* (London: SCM, 1971), 38–41.

9. Scholars are hesitant about including every little Matthew-Luke agreement in Q, because Q gets larger and larger and begins to resemble an alternative gospel to Mark, rather than a largely distinct collection of Jesus's sayings, as Q is usually thought to be.

Scholars favoring the two-source hypothesis have explained these agreements in a number of ways, including as simple coincidence or as due to textual corruption. Such suggestions are sometimes plausible enough. Yet, the alternative explanation of an oral tradition known to both Matthew and Luke seems to be an explanation of last resort, instead of being an obvious and highly plausible possibility. It is thoroughly credible that the saying about the purpose of parables was in the oral tradition known to Matthew and Luke, as indeed may be the case with the parables of the mustard seed and the leaven, which appear in Matthew in a version that is often ascribed to Q (Matt 13:31–33; Mark 4:30–32; Luke 13:18–21).[10] It is also thoroughly credible that the question of the soldiers was known to Matthew and Luke in oral tradition. Paul attests to the existence of a passion narrative in oral tradition.[11]

10. There is a case for thinking that Matthew and Luke had access to an early non-Markan version of much of the parabolic teaching found in Mark 4, Matt 13, and Luke 8. I noticed this evidence first in my 1970 doctoral thesis. For my more recent thinking, see David Wenham, "Matthean Priority: You Must Be Joking!" in *Treasures New and Old: Essays in Honor of Donald A. Hagner*, ed. Craig A. Evans, Cliff B. Kvidahl, and Matthew D. Montonini (Wilmore, KY: GlossaHouse, 2017).

11. The arguments about agreements of Matthew and Luke against Mark have been primarily addressing the two-source theory. And several of the observations made would be explained quite adequately by alternative views, e.g., by the view that Matthew was prior, or by the more fashionable view that Mark was known to Matthew and Luke, and that Luke also knew Matthew. These alternative views each have their weaknesses, for example in places where the Lukan version is arguably more "primitive" than the Matthean version (e.g. in the parable of the mustard seed). Bird, *The Gospel of the Lord*, highlights these difficulties and himself argues for Luke knowing a form of Q and also Matthew! See also Alan Garrow, "Streeter's 'Other' Synoptic Solution: The Matthew Conflator Hypothesis," *NTS* 62 (2016): 207–26. Both Bird and Goodacre, one of the most persuasive advo-

The presence of a strong oral tradition needs to be taken seriously. It should be a preferred explanation of the minor agreements and so-called Mark and Q overlaps.

---

cates of the Luke-used-Matthew view, acknowledge the importance of oral tradition but do not appear in practice to take it as a seriously major factor on the ground. Goodacre refers to Matthew and Luke interacting with it, resulting in more original wording than Mark "on occasion," *The Synoptic Problem: A Way through the Maze* (London: Sheffield Academic, 1996), 94. That is too cautious a recognition of the "default setting."

CHAPTER 6

Two Examples of the Oral Tradition

This chapter seeks to demonstrate from two passages that oral tradition offers persuasive explanation for the formation of the canonical gospels. As noted above, Paul attests the saying about the laborer being worthy of his hire (Matt 10:11 and Luke 10:7). This is widely ascribed to Q, as there are a number of agreements between Matthew and Luke against Mark in the mission discourses of Jesus. Luke, in fact, has two mission discourses, the first in Luke 9:1–9, addressed to the twelve, and the second in Luke 10:1–37, to the seventy. The first of these is most closely parallel to Mark 6:7–13, the second has more links with Matt 9:37–10:16. The common explanation is that Luke separated his Markan and Q sources, whereas Matthew has merged them in his account.[1] It is not necessary for

---

1. This is one of a number of "doublets" in Luke, where it is arguable that he has a Markan and non-Markan version of a story or saying. This particular case is complicated by the claim of Luke that there were two similar but distinct missions of disciples.

us to go into all the arguments for and against this view. What is notable is that Paul knew the saying about the laborer (and his readers probably did as well). As argued above, Paul probably knew not just the saying, but also some of its context with the apostles being sent out. If he did, where did he learn it?[2] The strong probability is that he knew it as part of the story of Jesus from oral tradition (1 Cor 11 and 15). If he did, then the Q hypothesis becomes redundant in this passage, since Matthew and Luke could also very well have known the oral tradition that Paul knew. Their divergences from Mark could reflect that knowledge.

There is a further interesting point to note about Paul and the discourse, relating particularly to the Matthean version of the discourse. One of the striking differences between Matthew on the one hand and Mark and Luke on the other is that Matthew has Jesus tell his disciples not to go to the Gentiles or the Samaritans "but only to the lost sheep of the house of Israel" (10:5–6). This has sometimes been seen as Matthew making Jesus more Jewish than he actually was, a redaction of the received material. Such an explanation is quite unlikely. Matthew is indeed distinctively Jewish in various ways, but he is clearly committed to Gentile mission, as is made clear at the end of the account (Matt 28:16–20).[3] It is much more probable

2. In theory, he might have known Q, if it existed; but that is a wholly speculative and redundant idea.

3. At the other end of the Gospel of Luke is the visit of the Gentile magi to worship Jesus (Matt 2:1–15). This not only tells against the view that 10:5 is a Matthean redaction, but also against the view that he imported it from a hypothetical source.

that the controversial command was part of the earliest tradition of Jesus's teaching about mission, which Mark and Luke—both probably writing for Gentiles—omitted. Paul may be a witness to the Matthean command, since he—though passionately committed to Gentile mission—is quite clear in his letters that the gospel is "for the Jew first, and also to the Greek" (Rom 1:16, etc.), that Jesus was a "servant to the circumcised" (Rom 15:8), and that Peter and the other disciples were sent specifically to the "circumcised" (Gal 2:7–9). The probability is that Matthew knew and was reflecting the Christian tradition that Paul also knew.[4] It is entirely plausible that Luke and probably Mark also knew this difficult saying of the Lord, though for obvious reasons they agree in omitting it.

Of course, Matt 10:5 can be explained on the standard literary explanations of the Synoptic Problem as M tradition: Matthew is drawing material from Mark, Q, and M. However, both Q and M are hypothetical, whereas Paul shows us that there was an oral tradition for this material. It probably included what scholars assign to different sources. There is every reason to suppose that Matthew, Mark, and Luke would have been familiar with that oral tradition. Oral tradition is a much simpler and more secure hypothesis than complicated literary relationships.[5]

4. It is interesting to speculate whether Paul's emphasis on making his gospel "free of charge" in 1 Cor 9:8 reflects the words in Matt 10:8, "Freely you have received, freely give." Compare 2 Cor 11:7 and 2 Thess 3:8–9. Note also Wenham, *Paul*, 197–98.

5. David Dungan finds the two-source theory seriously lacking in connection with the mission discourse; he argues that Matthew's form is

If Matt 10:5 can be sensibly explained in those terms, then that may well also be the case with Matt 15:24. Upon meeting a Canaanite woman, Jesus says of his own ministry, "I was not sent except to the lost sheep of the house of Israel." Paul may very well have known this saying. Note Rom 15:8 where Jesus is depicted as being a "servant of the circumcised." Mark may simply have omitted the saying.[6]

Above I argued there were other M traditions that Paul probably knew in the eschatological teaching of Jesus. Paul's comment in 1 Thess 5:2 about the Lord coming like a "thief in the night" is, as noted above, an echo of Jesus's parabolic saying, found in both Matthew and Luke (Matt 24:43; Luke 12:39). This saying is regularly seen as a Q tradition, but once again the strong evidence for an oral tradition, known and used by Paul, makes the hypothetical Q redundant, so far as this parable is concerned.[7] The evidence is wholly ex-

---

the most original, with Mark a "shortened, mutilated excerpt." See David Dungan, *The Sayings of Jesus in the Churches of Paul* (Oxford: Blackwell, 1971), 59–66, and Wenham, "Matthean Priority." There are various other places where Mark's discourse material may be seen as abbreviated paraphrases of a longer tradition that was probably known to Matthew: see Mark 13:33–37, also perhaps 12:38–40.

6. Mark still has the potentially embarrassing saying about not taking the children's bread and giving it to the dogs (Mark 7:27), but the offensive point is not explicit as it is in the omitted saying. Another conspicuously Jewish saying is in Matt 18:17 in the discourse about the church. This chapter is mostly unique to Matthew. Interestingly there are possible connections between the M material of the chapter and 1 Cor 5:3–5; see Roy E. Ciampa and Brian S. Rosner, *The First Letter to the Corinthians* (Nottingham: Apollos, 2010), 206–7, and also Wenham, *Paul*, 210–13.

7. Of course, it could be that Q was drawing on the same oral tradition as Paul, which would be a testimony to the early date of the tra-

plicable in terms of the evangelists knowing the same oral tradition as Paul.

The parable of the thief is followed in both Matthew and Luke by the parable of the faithful and unfaithful stewards (Matt 24:45–51; Luke 12:41–46), which scholars regularly ascribe to Q. Might it too have simply belonged to oral tradition?[8]

The next parable in Matthew is that of the wise and foolish virgins (Matt 25:1–13). There is a good case for Paul alluding to it in 1 Thess 4. It might be the "word of the Lord" that he uses to address the anxieties of the Thessalonians about "those who have fallen asleep." The parable is found only in Matthew's Gospel. It is labeled M by source critics. Yet, Paul's evidence points to it being part of the same oral tradition that he knew.[9]

Matthew's next parable is that of the talents (25:14–30), often labeled as Q material because a very similar parable appears in Luke, albeit in a different context (Luke 19:12–27). Again the question is: Was the talents in the oral tradition?[10]

---

dition, since Q is thought to have been written in the 40s or 50s CE. But the Pauline evidence does make the Q hypothesis redundant so far as this parable is concerned.

8. Paul may have that parable in mind in 1 Cor 4:1–4, where he speaks of stewards of Christ being "found faithful" and being judged by the "lord" or "master."

9. It is possible that Luke shows knowledge of the parable of the virgins in 12:35—i.e., in the same group of sayings as the thief and the stewards—since he has Jesus say "Let your loins be girded and your lamps burning." Scholars mostly label that saying as L material, but perhaps it is an echo of the parable that Matthew and Paul attest.

10. The closest parallel in Paul to the parable of the talents is probably in his discussion of gifts in 1 Cor 12, where he speaks of different gifts being given to the members of the church.

The overall picture relating to Matthew and Luke is as follows. Matthew 24–25 has: (1) parable of the thief (parallels in Luke, and Paul); (2) parable of the stewards (parallels in Luke, and perhaps Paul [1 Cor 4:1–4]); (3) parable of the virgins (parallels probably in Paul, and perhaps hinted at in Luke 12:35); (4) parable of the talents (parallel possible in Luke). Luke 12 includes (1) a possibly echo of parable of virgins in 12:35, also in Matthew and Paul; (2) the parable of the servants keeping watch (no parallel in Matthew; but possible echo in Matt 24:42 "Keep awake then, for you do not know in what day your lord is coming," especially if the manuscripts with "hour" rather than "day" are preferred; (3) Parable of the thief (parallels in Luke and Paul); (4) Peter's question "Lord, are you saying this parable to us or also to all?"; (5) Parable of stewards (parallels in Matthew, and perhaps Paul).

Scholars have regularly concluded that there was a group of eschatological parables, used by Matthew in chapters 24–25 and by Luke in 12:35-48. This conclusion seems probable, but the evidence of Paul points in the direction of oral tradition, not Q. Also, the parable of the virgins has a claim to be included in the group, even though it is not in Luke. The saying in Luke 12:35—"let your loins be girded and your lamps lit"—could be a hint that Luke knows the parable. Luke has another parable in his collection, namely the parable of the servants waiting for their master's return from a wedding at some unspecified hour of the night (12:35-38).[11] This parable too must be a candi-

---

11. It is possible that the reference to returning from the wedding

date for inclusion in a collection of parables, and possibly also the question from Peter following the parable of the thief: "Lord, are you saying this parable to us or also to all?" (12:41), a question to which no direct answer is given.

The argument for such an oral tradition is greatly strengthened by the evidence of Mark 13:33–37. Scholars have often noted links with parables in Matthew and Luke. However, they have not seen their full significance. Indeed, the relationships have, understandably, been something of a puzzle to scholars. There is, however, a straightforward explanation. It is helpful to have a rather literal translation of Mark 13:33–37:

- Mark 13:33 Watch out, keep awake. For you do not know when the moment is.
- Mark 13:34 (It is) like a man leaving his house to go away and giving his servants authority to each his work, and to the doorkeeper he commanded that he keep awake.
- Mark 13:35 Keep awake then; for you do not know when the master of the house is coming, whether late or at midnight or at cockcrow or very early.
- Mark 13:36 Otherwise, coming suddenly he finds you sleeping.
- What I say to you I say to all, keep awake.

These Markan verses make their point very clearly about the importance of staying awake, but they read

at night is somehow related to the parable of the wise and foolish virgins. See also Luke 13:25.

disjointedly. Mark 13:34 sounds like the beginning of the parable of the talents in Matthew's Gospel where the master goes away on a journey and gives certain responsibilities to each of his servants. But the story in Mark is very different. The Gospel of Mark focuses on one person—the doorkeeper—and his job. This sounds like the beginning of the parable found in Luke 12:35–38 about the master going to a wedding and appointing his servants to open the door when he returns, at whatever watch of the night (though there is one doorkeeper in Mark not a group of servants as in Luke). In Mark, the parable is not developed. Rather, we switch in Mark 13:35–36 from the third person story of the master, his servants, and the doorkeeper to second-person exhortation from Jesus. This applies the parable of the doorkeeper to the disciples, before applying it "to all." The words of the Lord here in Mark, "What I say to you, I say to all," sound intriguingly like a reply to Peter's question in Luke 12:41, "Lord, do you say this parable to us or to all?"

What is going on here? What should one make of the possible links of Mark with the Matthean and Lukan parables? It is theoretically possible that Matthew has been following Mark for most of Jesus's eschatological discourse, but when he reaches the somewhat ungainly Mark 13:33–37, he largely abandons Mark and creates an alternative ending with the help of Q and other material. However, that is a rather complicated solution[12] that does

12. See the circumspect discussion by W. D. Davies and Dale Allison, *The Gospel according to Saint Matthew*, Vol. 3 (Edinburgh: T&T Clark, 1997), 375. They see Matthew as following Mark until Mark 13:32, then turning to

not explain the Markan verses—either their disjointed-ness or their particular links to both Matthew and Luke.[13] The preferable explanation of the relationships at this point is that Mark, Matthew, and Luke are all drawing on a common oral tradition in different ways, with Mark's disjointedness due to his abbreviated and compressed use of the tradition that is more fully represented in Matthew and Luke.[14]

It is, of course, not only Mark who has made selec-tive use of the oral tradition. Matthew has done the same, omitting the parable of the watchman or watchmen at-tested in both Mark and Luke. Luke omits the parable of the virgins, attested by Matthew and Paul.

This oral explanation represents a straightforward explanation of the different texts, whereas purely lit-erary accounts of their relationships struggle here.[15] It is plausible, not least because we know that some such oral tradition of Jesus's eschatological parables existed (as

---

Q, then back to Mark 13:35, then back to Q, then to oral tradition (note!) for the parable of the virgins, and then back to Q for the parable of the talents.

13. The similarity of the wording of Luke's question in 12:41, "Lord are you telling this parable to us or to all?" and the saying in Mark 13:37, "What I say to you I say to all, keep awake," is not even noted by some commentators, let alone seen as significant. It may seem bizarre to have the question in Luke and the answer in Mark. However, such an interpre-tation makes very good sense given the oral explanation.

14. There is much fuller discussion of the eschatological material in Wenham, *Paul*, 305–37. See also David Wenham, *The Rediscovery of Jesus' Eschatological Discourse* (Sheffield: JSOT, 1984), in which I argued in detail for a pre-synoptic oral form of the discourse.

15. For this sort of view of Mark 13:33–37, see G. R. Beasley-Murray, *A Commentary on Mark 13* (London: Macmillan, 1957), 11–12; Jan Lambrecht, *Die Redaktion der Markus-Apokalypse* (Rome: Pontifical Institute, 1967), 249–51.

attested by Paul), whereas Q is hypothetical and indeed redundant in this case.[16]

It is not just the eschatological parables that are explicable in terms of such oral tradition; as noted above, the parallels between the canonical gospels and Paul's description of the Lord's coming are not limited to these parables. In 1 Thess 4, Paul refers to the Lord coming from heaven "with a cry of command, with the voice of an archangel, and with the trumpet of God," and meeting up with his people, living and departed (4:13–18). The passage is strongly reminiscent of the portrayal of Jesus's coming on the clouds with his angels to gather his elect in Matt 24, Mark 13, and Luke 21. Once again it seems likely that a common oral tradition explains these parallels.

Some parallels are between versions of the teaching of the Lord in Paul and Matthew.[17] There are also some Lukan traditions: his ending of the eschatological discourse in Luke 21:34–36 is distinctive with its warnings about the coming of "that day," which will "come upon" you "suddenly" . . . keep awake . . . that you may

---

16. The intriguing parallel sayings in Didache 16 are explained, rather improbably in my view, by Alan Garrow, *The Gospel of Matthew's Dependence on the Didache*, JSNTSup 254 (London: T&T Clark, 2004), 216, who argues that Matthew used parts of the Didache. Note also Alan Garrow, "The Eschatological Tradition behind 1 Thessalonians: Didache 16," *JSNT* 32 (2009): 191–215. Didache 16:1 is interestingly similar to the Matthean parable of the virgins and to the following passage in Luke 12:35: "Keep awake for the sake of your life. And let your lamps not be extinguished, and your loins not ungirded, but be ready, for you do not know the hour, in which your lord is coming." Garrow does not notice or discuss the possible Pauline use of the parable of the virgins in 1 Thess 4. The Didache may well be a further witness to the earliest oral traditions.

17. E.g., the sound of the trumpet.

have strength to "escape." Paul in 1 Thess 5:2–4 speaks about "the day of the Lord coming" . . . then "sudden" destruction "comes on" them, and they will not "escape." Relatively unusual Greek words are used in both (notably *aiphnidios*, "sudden" or "suddenly"). The warnings and exhortations in both passages are very similar ("don't get drunk" . . . "keep awake"). The parallels themselves do not prove anything. And yet the warnings in Paul are immediately adjacent to the verse about the thief in the night, where Paul is using an oral tradition of Jesus's eschatological teaching. The presence of such a tradition is again possible.[18]

What is striking is that in 1 Thess 4–5 one finds what scholars identify as Markan tradition (the coming on clouds with angels), Q (the thief), M (the wise and foolish girls, the trumpet), and possibly L (the warnings against dissipation in face of the sudden inescapable judgment). From a traditional source-critical viewpoint it might possibly seem surprising that M and L traditions are known to Paul and are there alongside Q and Markan sayings. If the default position among scholars was oral tradition, then there is no problem or indeed surprise in what we have observed, since Paul and the authors of the synop-

---

18. 2 Thess 2 is another passage where there are striking similarities between the Pauline teaching and the synoptic eschatological teaching. The warnings against excessive excitement, deceivers, and deceptive signs, the description of the man of lawlessness and of his destruction by the Lord when he comes are all paralleled in Mark 13, Matt 24, and Luke 21. The "desolating sacrilege" and the "lawless one" have a common background in Daniel and the events of 167 BCE associated with Antiochus Epiphanes. See Wenham, *Paul*, 316–19.

tic gospels are drawing in different ways on that shared tradition.

The different examples given of texts where there is a case for oral tradition have not all been equally strong. However, the main examples from the mission discourse and the eschatological discourse are persuasive evidence for an oral tradition known to the three Synoptic Gospels and to Paul. The oral hypothesis makes good sense, where traditional literary explanations are less than persuasive.[19] It would be possible to extend the argument to many other passages.[20] The evidence presented here effectively

19. In both the mission discourse material and the eschatological material, I have argued that the Q hypothesis, as usually conceived, becomes questionable. Paul attests the existence of an oral tradition including what scholars have identified as Q material (i.e., the laborer's reward saying and the thief saying). In addition, the oral tradition contained not just sayings common to Matthew and Luke but also M and L material. In theory, one might expand the definition of Q to include all the sayings, but it makes more sense in these contexts—although not necessarily in others—to dispense with the hypothetical Q and to reference oral tradition.

20. There is good reason to think that Paul knew of so-called M traditions in the mission discourses (e.g., the saying about not going to the Gentiles) and in the eschatological teaching (e.g., the parable of the virgins). There are other examples where the same situation may be the case. For example, it is quite possible that Paul in Gal 1 and 2 has in mind Jesus's congratulation of Peter as recorded only in Matt 16:15–17. After Peter's confession of Jesus as "the Christ, the Son of the living God," Jesus replies: "Blessed are you, Simon Bar-Jona, because flesh and blood have not revealed this to you but my Father who is in heaven. And I tell you that you are Peter, and on this rock I will build my church." In Gal 1–2, Paul defends his apostleship (in order to defend his gospel), probably in response to those who questioned it and compared him unfavorably with Peter. Paul's response includes a very direct comparison of himself with Peter (2:7 "just as Peter"). Paul knows that Peter was very specifically chosen by Jesus as an apostle ("to the circumcised," 2:8), and in speaking of his own calling, Paul uses terms similar to those used by Jesus of Peter in Matt 16;

demonstrates the utility of oral traditions in explaining the canonical gospels.[21]

---

so he speaks very specifically of God "revealing his Son" (1:16, also 1:12, "a revelation of Jesus Christ"), of not consulting "flesh and blood" (1:16), and of the purpose of this revelation being for mission and apostleship (1:16). Paul does not, of course, speak of himself being a rock on which Christ will build his church, but he does believe that he has been given a comparable role to Peter, albeit to the uncircumcised. It is an attractive possibility that Paul knew the M tradition. If he knew the congratulatory saying, did he also know its context and Peter's confession? Most scholars assume that Matthew is using Mark in his summary of the confession (Mark 8:29: "You are the Christ"; Matt 16:16: "You are the Christ, the Son of the living God" [compare Luke 9:20: "the Christ of God"]) and then added the congratulatory reply of Jesus to Peter, where Mark has no such reply. Rather, Mark includes an abrupt warning. This sounds plausible, and yet Mark is famously hard on the disciples, including Peter. He could have wanted to move on directly to the first prediction of Jesus's passion and not to dwell on the great confession of Peter and what it represented. A rigid adherence to Markan priority and literary explanations of the relationships between the Synoptic Gospels makes it almost unthinkable that Matthew might here have the earlier original form of the tradition. However, if the existence and importance of oral tradition are taken seriously, Matthean priority in the confession is entirely possible. Matthew may be using Mark and oral tradition, here, as in Matt 10. For further discussion of the possible links between Galatians and Matthew, see Wenham, *Paul*, 200–205. Robert H. Gundry, *Peter: False Disciples and Apostate according to Saint Matthew* (Grand Rapids: Eerdmans, 2015), 17, notes but does not discuss the possible parallel between Gal 1:15–17 and Matt 16:16–20. His argument that the congratulation of Peter in Matthew is half-hearted or worse—since the revelation was necessary because of his obtuseness—is unpersuasive; both Peter in Matthew and Peter and Paul in Galatians are greatly privileged and given important roles by God.

21. J. D. G. Dunn discusses some passages where he thinks oral tradition to be the evangelists' source in *The Oral Gospel Tradition* (Grand Rapids: Eerdmans, 2013), 63–73. He tends to identify passages where the similarity is not too exact, which is understandable, although the close agreement can also be the result of oral tradition. In parallel passages, the default assumption should not be Markan priority. Rather, oral traditions preserved in Matthew and Luke may represent earlier versions of traditions about Jesus.

CHAPTER 7

The Extent of the Oral Tradition

In the previous chapters we have seen that Paul attests to a variety of traditions about Jesus and that oral tradition makes sense in reading the texts of the canonical gospels. Each of the evangelists drew upon oral tradition. It is impossible to establish the precise contents and contours of the oral tradition. Evidently, it included sayings of the Lord and probably some discourse material (e.g., mission and eschatological discourses). It may have included a version of the Sermon on the Mount or Sermon on the Plain: scholars have often explained the parallels between Matthew and Luke in terms of Q.[1] However, it is quite feasible that the explanation is via oral tradition and Paul was familiar with it.[2]

---

1. The fact that Mark does not have the sermon does not count as a valid objection against its presence in the early oral tradition. Mark is explicit about being selective with his teaching material (see 4:33; 12:38). The Gospel of Mark focuses on the mighty deeds and then the passion of Jesus; he was not writing an account in the same way as Matthew or even Luke. Mark has a strong narrative focus that drives the story forward.

2. Contra Luz, "The Use of Jesus-Traditions in the Pauline and Post-

The oral tradition also included an extended narrative—of the passion and resurrection. And it is entirely possible that it included other narrative relating to Jesus. Although it sometimes seems to be a scholarly "given" that the sayings of Jesus were transmitted without a narrative framework, it is quite likely that some sayings like the divorce teaching of Jesus were remembered in their context (in that particular case, the context of people questioning him about divorce). Defenders of the Q hypothesis have to allow that Q was not sayings material alone. The account of John the Baptist, a recognized portion of Q, includes narrative material. If this is a minor embarrassment for the Q hypothesis, it is in no way an embarrassment for the hypothesis of an early and extensive oral tradition. The story of John the Baptist in Matthew and Luke can be explained as an instance of overlap between Mark and the oral tradition.

The oral tradition probably contained accounts of various stories of Jesus's pre-passion life, including the sending out of the twelve and other traditions connected with the apostles. Luz is one of a number of scholars who argue that Paul and his readers knew about Jesus's hum-

---

Pauline Letters," 89, and others. It is also feasible in relation to other discourses. For example, scholars have often postulated the existence of an early pre-Markan collection of Jesus's parables. It seems probable, in this case, that Matthew, Mark, and Luke are all drawing on an early oral tradition. The evidence includes the minor agreements of Matthew and Luke in the saying on the purpose of parables (Mark 4:10–11 and parallels), the Mark and Q overlap in the parable of the mustard seed (Mark 4:30–32 and Luke 13:18–19), and the clumsiness of Mark in that parable. See Wenham, "The Priority of Matthew."

ble lifestyle and humility, as a model to be imitated, noting Phil 2; 2 Cor 8:9; 1 Thess 1:6; 2 Cor 10:1.[3]

There is even an argument that Paul knows a version of the infancy stories of Jesus, however unlikely this may sound. Paul's words in Gal 4:4 ("When the fullness of time had come, God sent forth his Son, born of a woman, born under the law, to redeem those under the Law") have intriguing resonance with the Lukan account of the birth of Jesus with the almost tangible excitement there over the imminent coming of Jesus the Savior in fulfillment of God's promises of redemption for Israel (Luke 1:68), the story of Jesus's birth as "Son of God" to a virgin, who had not "known a man" (Luke 1:34),[4] and the specific description of the infant Jesus being brought to the temple to do everything commanded by the Law (Luke 2:22–27). It has also been noted that the Greek verb Paul uses the normal Greek word *gennaomai* of natural begetting and being born when referring to Jacob and Ishmael in Gal 4:33–34, but when referring to Jesus in Gal 4:4 he chooses the verb *ginomai* (with its broad semantic range, including "come to be" and so "be born").[5] Paul uses the same verb of Jesus's birth also in Phil 2:7 and Rom 1:3.[6]

3. Luz, "The Use of Jesus-Traditions in the Pauline and Post-Pauline Letters," 85–86.

4. Paul's "born of a woman" does not imply virginal conception of course, but the specific reference to his mother is notable.

5. GE, 429.

6. See on this C. E. B. Cranfield, "Some Reflections on the Subject of the Virgin Birth," *SJT* 41 (1988): 177–98. For a major treatment of the subject of the virgin birth, rejecting this view, see Andrew Lincoln, *Born of a Virgin?* (Grand Rapids: Eerdmans, 2013), 22. Lincoln's comment that the verb *ginomai* can be used of normal human birth proves nothing; he

The suggestion that Paul knew the tradition of Jesus's birth attested in Luke deserves more credence than is often given. But even if it is rejected, the other less speculative evidence points to the earliest oral traditions of Jesus being extensive, covering the Jesus story from John the Baptist (if not earlier) to the resurrection. Some of them, at least, were collected together, for example, the passion narrative and the eschatological parables. Is there any reason to suppose that there was anything like a complete oral narrative of Jesus's life and ministry? There are reasons for thinking so. First, it seems unlikely that there were many known and valued traditions of the Lord that were not brought together. People would want to know the big story of what led up to "the night when he was betrayed." Second, there is the evidence particularly from the book of Acts. This evidence suggests that proclaiming the gospel to someone like Cornelius included telling the story of Jesus from John the Baptist to the resurrection. The job of the apostles was telling people the story and stories. Third, there is the evidence of the written canonical gospels themselves. They may plausibly be seen as written versions of what they received (not, as is often imagined, the development of a quite new form of connected narrative). Luke certainly seems to be making this

---

does not observe that Paul uses *ginomai* in Gal 4:4 of Jesus but *gennaomai* just a few verses later in Gal 4:21–31 of Isaac and Esau. His observation that Paul sees Jesus as of David's and Abraham's "seed" to the exclusion of the virgin birth is unpersuasive. Matthew and Luke in their accounts of the virgin birth also see Jesus as of the house and lineage of Abraham and David. Lincoln fails to notice the general similarity of Gal 4:4–5 to the Lukan infancy narrative.

claim. He views it as the sort of good news that the early Christian community proclaimed. The other evangelists imply something similar. Fourth, there is more evidence from Paul. He begins his letter to the Romans by introducing himself as an apostle set apart for the gospel of God. He then offers a sort of summary of that gospel (1:1–5):

> *which he promised beforehand through his prophets in the holy Scriptures, concerning*
> his Son,
> born of the seed of David according to the flesh
> marked out as Son of God in power according to the Spirit of holiness through resurrection of the dead,
> Jesus Christ our Lord,
> *through whom we received grace and apostleship for the obedience of faith among all the nations.*

Scholars have often argued that this is a pre-Pauline creedal fragment. Whether that is the case or not, the verses serve in this letter to the Romans as Paul's first summary of the good news that he proclaimed as an apostle. It summarizes the story of Jesus, referring to its Old Testament background, to the life of Jesus from his birth through to his resurrection,[7] and to the ongoing apostolic proclamation of Jesus among the nations.

7. Being "born" of the seed of David is the Greek verb *ginomai*, which often means "become"; the translation could be "coming from the seed of David." But see our earlier comment on the possibility of Paul knowing the story of Jesus's virginal conception.

It is interesting to compare this with the other summary of the good news in 1 Cor 15:1: "I want you to know, brothers, the gospel which I proclaimed to you, which also you received . . . I passed on to you as of first importance, which I also received, that Christ died for our sins according to the Scriptures, and that he was buried and that he was raised on the third day according to the Scriptures, and that he appeared." 1 Corinthians differs from Romans in that there is no reference to the birth of Jesus. But that is entirely explicable. In 1 Cor 15, Paul is addressing the question of resurrection, and so his summary of the good news is shaped accordingly and the pre-crucifixion story of Jesus is irrelevant in that context.

We are reminded not to see these possibly creedal passages as anything like full creeds; they are summaries. And, if 1 Cor 15 focuses on the resurrection, Gal 4:4—another candidate for recognition as a creedal statement—focuses on his incarnation: "In the fullness of time God sent forth his Son." The "hymn" of Phil 2:5–11 refers both to Jesus's assuming human form and to his crucifixion and resurrection.

A final observation about Rom 1:1–5 is in order. The shape of Paul's description of the gospel here is intriguingly like the shape of Matthew's Gospel in particular:[8]

8. See Idicheria Ninan, *Jesus as the Son of God: An Examination of the Background and Meaning of "Son of God" in Paul's Christology with Particular Reference to Romans 8* (PhD diss., Coventry University, 1994), 176–78. Richard Hays, *The Faith of Jesus Christ: An Investigation of the Narrative Substructure of Galatians 3:1–4:11* (Chico: Scholars, 1983), 257, argues that Paul knew an outline of the story of Jesus (as seen in verses like Gal 3:13 and 4:4–5). This suggests

- starting with the Old Testament (compare Rom 1:2, "which he promised before through his prophets in the holy Scriptures," and Matthew's genealogy in chapter 1, linking Jesus to the story of Israel from Abraham to David to Jesus himself),
- continuing with the story of Jesus from his birth to his resurrection,
- and concluding with an emphasis on the gospel going to all nations (compare "we received apostleship and grace to bring about obedience of faith among all the nations for his name's sake" with Matt 28:19 "going, make disciples of all the nations, baptizing them in the name of the Father and the Son and the Holy Spirit, teaching them to keep all these things that I commanded you"). Luke's Gospel is quite similar with a strong Old Testament orientation in chs. 1–2 and a commissioning to evangelize all the nations in Jesus's name in 24:46–49.[9]

What did Paul say about Jesus when bringing the good news to people in different places? We conclude that there is good reason to believe that the good news that

---

that such an outline story could have contributed to the development of the accounts in Matthew, Mark, Luke, and John. It could be the other way round (i.e., Paul knows and is influenced by the oral tradition).

9. If it was Paul's practice to explain the gospel in those terms, one might guess that it was also the practice of those who worked with him and continued the work of "telling the good news" (cf. Eph 4:11 on the gift of "evangelist," or good-newser). The evidence of Acts, if the author was a companion of Paul, entirely supports this guess. The book of Acts says that John Mark also spent time in Paul's team, quite probably also sharing in ministry of explaining the good news to people.

they brought was the story of Jesus, not just pithy creedal statements or disconnected stories. The story of Jesus was likely a complete narrative (or narratives) giving a rather comprehensive account of his life and ministry, not dissimilar to what we find in Matthew, Mark, Luke, and John.[10]

10. Stephen Hultgren, *Narrative Elements in the Double Tradition: A Study of Their Place within the Framework of the Gospel Narrative* (Berlin: Walter de Gruyter, 2002), makes an important argument for there being coherent pre-Markan oral narrative traditions, which Matthew and Luke use from time to time. His argument involves a careful engagement with various solutions of the synoptic problem, pointing out their inadequacies. He does not bring out the evidence of Paul, which would only strengthen his well-made case.

CHAPTER 8

The Message of the First Christians

As quoted earlier, Stanton writes:

> It must have been all but impossible to avoid
> sketching out the life and character of Jesus in
> missionary proclaiming. How could one claim
> that Jesus was the one person in the whole of
> history who fulfilled scripture in its widest and
> deepest sense, that Jesus was raised from the
> dead by God in a totally unexpected and unique
> way, and call for repentance and commitment to
> him without indicating who he was? How could
> one mention the crucifixion without answer-
> ing in anticipation careful questioning about
> the events which led to the rejection of Jesus?
> Could one begin to mention the betrayal, arrest
> and trial of Jesus without arousing interest in the
> teachings and actions of Jesus?[1]

1. Stanton, *Jesus of Nazareth in New Testament Preaching*, 176–77. Note

This book argues that what Stanton said "must have been" did in fact happen. The results of this journey through a maze of evidence and scholarly discussion can be summed up:

1. The evidence is clear that from very early in the history of the church there was a strong oral tradition of the sayings and stories of Jesus. Not all the detailed arguments for such tradition that have been discussed are equally strong. Yet, the overall weight of evidence is sufficient to justify describing it as overwhelming. There is the evidence of our primary historical source for the beginnings of the church (Acts). There is the evidence of our first written accounts of Jesus's life and teaching (Matthew, Mark, Luke, and John). They all suggest that they are doing in writing what had been going on orally before, when "the good news" of Jesus was preached and taught. There is the evidence of our earliest New Testament author, Paul, who shows that oral tradition was of primary importance. There is evidence of the different accounts. These texts are inadequately explained in purely literary terms.
2. The tradition was very extensive, including a wide range of different traditions that are found in the canonical gospels (e.g., passion and resurrection narratives, parables, eschatological and ethical teaching, and stories about Jesus).

also Graham Stanton, *The Gospels and Jesus* (Oxford: Oxford University Press, 1989).

3. The oral tradition was not just individual sayings or stories. It was something much more extensive, like the canonical gospels. It was not just a case of "floating logia," as scholars sometimes call them. Rather, it included connected narratives (e.g., the passion), blocks of teaching (e.g., eschatological parables), and also some sayings in the context of narrative (e.g., the mission discourse).[2] Peter's speech to Cornelius and his family in Acts 10 summarizes the entire story of Jesus in a nutshell. C. H. Dodd argued years ago that the speech resembles Mark's Gospel in outline.[3] Paul's description of the gospel in Rom 1:1–4 is intriguingly similar to the shape of Matthew in particular.

4. The oral tradition included stories about Jesus that have been labeled by modern critics as Markan, Q, M, L, and even Johannine traditions. Many scholars have recognized that Paul has some "Markan tradition" (or the "triple tradition").[4] There are also echoes of

2. Luz, "The Use of Jesus-Traditions in the Pauline and Post-Pauline Letters," 89, expresses doubt about whether Paul knew cycles of teaching. He asserts that "the sermon on the Mount/Plain did not yet exist." This confident assertion is not justified but probably reflects his background as a scholar who reads Matthew as a redaction critic. He argues that 1 Peter presupposes Matthew's Gospel and knows Matthean redactional elements (in 1 Pet 2:12 and 3:14, drawing on Matt 5:16). Remarkably, he says that Matthew was not used as a source text, but rather a "secondary oralization of Jesus-tradition on the basis of the text of the first Gospel." It must be simpler to think of Matthew and 1 Peter drawing on the early oral tradition.

3. Compare C. H. Dodd, *The Apostolic Preaching and Its Developments* (London: Hodder, 1936), 54–56, 104–17.

4. E.g., his references to divorce, the second coming, and Jesus's use of "Abba."

so-called Q tradition.[5] As noted above, Paul was also familiar with distinctively Matthean and Lukan material, and probably even some Johannine tradition. This conclusion is wholly unsurprising given all the arguments about the early oral tradition.

5. All our evangelists and Paul knew such oral traditions and have often drawn on them in different ways.[6]

What are the implications? The consequences of these observations are noteworthy: Scholars have struggled for centuries to solve the Synoptic problem and to explain the relationship of Matthew, Mark, and Luke. The rediscovery of the oral tradition complicates the issue in some ways. There was a certain simplicity in explaining everything in terms of four sources (i.e., Mark, Q, and the special material in Matthew and Luke). But now we no longer can have confidence that Mark has the most original version of a story or a saying, or that Matthew and Luke (if they used Mark) have a less original version. The opposite may be the case: Matthew or Luke may have followed the early oral tradition rather than Mark . However, if in some ways the rediscovery of oral tradition complicates things, in other ways it helps enormously by offering solutions to problems that traditional source criticism could not adequately address.[7] The recognition of the great importance

5. E.g., the sayings about the laborer and the thief.
6. Other writers—such as the authors of 1 Peter, James, and the Didache—did the same.
7. So Dunn, *Oral Tradition*, 76.

and influence of oral tradition in no way excludes literary relationships between the canonical gospels. However, it does mean that literary explanations are not adequate in and of themselves.[8] Q is a hazardous hypothetical document, as many scholars have noted over the years. There is no external evidence of Q (no manuscript or reference in the early church). Its supporters have reconstructed it with great confidence. But the enterprise is speculative. It has been identified as a collection of Jesus's sayings.[9] However, this supposed collection is not purely sayings. Rather, it begins with the ministry of John the Baptist and goes on to Jesus's three temptations in the desert and his exorcisms. The uncomfortable fact is that Q is a scholars' deduction from evidence that can otherwise be explained—though that in itself does not necessarily mean that it is a wrong deduction.

Some scholars have postulated Q as oral tradition, or several collections of oral tradition.[10] This observation moves in the direction of the argument of this book, though the result is much closer to an oral gospel, including the narrative traditions that Paul received and passed on.

Many scholars appeal to the very high level of verbal agreement between Matthew and Luke in some of the Q passages, which seems to demand a literary explanation:

8. Two of the recent and strong advocates of the priority of oral tradition, namely Dunn and Bird, accept both Markan priority and the existence of some sort of Q, as did Stanton.

9. The Gospel of Thomas is such a collection.

10. Most scholars who speak of an M and L source would probably also think of them as oral traditions available to Matthew and Luke.

either there was a Q document or Luke knew Matthew, as some have forcefully argued. But this common argument makes a very questionable, although very widespread, assumption about oral tradition being much less reliable than written tradition. Today, it is hard for us to imagine oral tradition being as accurate as written records. The assumption is understandable for those of us who live in a literary culture. Books and electronic resources store information; human memory is less important. However, in non- or semi-literary cultures things were and are very different. Memorization lies at the heart of communication, teaching, and learning. In such contexts, people remember things with startling accuracy and tenacity. That was the case in Jesus's context, where schooling was based on memorizing, where people learned the Scriptures by heart, and where the rabbis taught so that their teaching could be memorized and learned, which it was to a very high degree.[11] There is no reason why the level of similarity found in various passages may not mostly be explained via oral tradition rather than literary trans-

---

11. Cf. Gerhardson, *Memory and Manuscript*. He has been followed by various others, including Riesner, *Jesus als Lehrer*. Baum, *Der mündliche Faktor und seine Bedeutung für die synoptische Frage*, 416, comments on the extraordinary feats of memory achieved by Jewish scholars, learning the whole of the Old Testament and much rabbinic tradition, and says: "Not least because of its moderate length, it was possible for the disciples of Jesus to store the whole synoptic tradition in memory, even without the benefit of rabbinic education and training." Recently Travis Derico, *Oral Tradition and the Synoptic Verbal Agreement Evaluating the Empirical Evidence for Literary Dependence* (Eugene, OR: Pickwick, 2016), comments on how again and again scholars assume that close or identical wording must indicate a written source. He offers a forceful argument against our modern assumption that oral tradition cannot be very accurate.

mission.[12] There is every reason to believe that the early Christians would have transmitted the good news of Jesus—the stories and the sayings—with care and that the authors of Matthew, Mark, Luke, and John (as well as Paul) would have known those oral traditions.

Although this conclusion must be of importance in discussion of the Synoptic problem, it is not the purpose of this book to argue for any particular solution. Some scholars in the past have argued that all the canonical gospels were written independently based on oral tradition, without any literary dependence.[13] That is not what is being argued here. The case for Matthew and Luke knowing Mark remains a strong one. However, Luke's prologue with its reference to "many" having undertaken to put together an account does not necessarily mean that there were many written accounts. It is quite likely that there were various writings, with Mark being the one we know.[14] It is possible that there was a written Q of some

12. Agreements in order (not just wording) are also often cited as evidence of literary rather than oral tradition. It is hard for us to imagine whole discourses or narratives being taught and learned. If there was some passing on of Jesus traditions, it would have been systematic, not material in one order this week and in another order next week.

13. Some scholars have backed away from literary explanations: Bo Reicke, *The Roots of the Synoptic Gospels* (Philadelphia: Fortress, 1986); John Rist, *On the Independence of Matthew and Mark* (Cambridge: Cambridge University Press, 2005); Baum, *Der mündliche Faktor und seine Bedeutung für die synoptische Frage*.

14. Rainer Riesner argues for a complex history of the transmission of Jesus traditions in his important article "The Orality and Memory Hypothesis," in *The Synoptic Problem: Four Views*, ed. Stanley E. Porter and Bryan R. Dyer (Grand Rapids: Baker, 2016), 89–111, 151–63. The idea that even during his ministry disciples might have made written notes is not completely unthinkable; see E. Earle Ellis, *Christ and the Future in New Tes-*

sort.[15] Although, as argued above, much of what has been explained in terms of lost literary sources is just as well explained via oral tradition. But the intention of this book is not to solve the Synoptic problem. Rather, the intention is to argue that one should never imagine Matthew or Luke (or whoever) writing their gospels simply on the basis of one or two literary sources; oral traditions about Jesus were known and widely circulated. Matthew and Luke knew a lot of non-Markan versions of sayings and stories of Jesus, some of them attested also by Paul. They were drawing on oral tradition.

The importance of the argument for reading the canonical gospels is considerable. If Matthew and Luke did not only have Mark, but pre-Markan traditions, and if indeed these pre-Markan traditions were often the original source of their knowledge, this will mean (1) that their departures from Mark may reflect the oral sources, and may be more original than Mark, not Matthew's or Luke's secondary editing, and (2) that when they do follow Mark's wording and story, they often compared

---

tament History, NovTSup 97 (Leiden: Brill, 2001), 212–41. Francis Watson refers to Mark using earlier text forms, and indeed speaks of "an editorial chain extending back into the obscure origins of gospel writing," in his article "How Did Mark Survive?" in *Matthew and Mark across Perspectives: Essays in Honour of Stephen C. Barton and William R. Telford*, ed. Kristian A. Bendoraitis and Nijay K. Gupta (London: T&T Clark, 2016), 2–6. But the evidence he produces for pre-Markan traditions is better explained via oral traditions.

15. I am not excluding other views, e.g., that Luke may have known Matthew (or vice versa). What I am arguing against is what could be described as the captivity of New Testament scholarship to literary explanations, which prevents many scholars from taking the priority and importance of the oral tradition seriously.

the Markan version with pre-Markan information. They must presumably have judged Mark to be reliable in those cases, which is hardly surprising if it is true that all the evangelists, including Mark, were using shared oral traditions, albeit in different ways.[16]

The argument put forward has important implications not just for the reading of the canonical gospels, but also for the study of Paul's letters and of other parts of the New Testament. It means that scholars should be more alert to echoes of Jesus in Paul;[17] minimalism in this matter—including when it comes to the possibility of Paul using M, L, and Johannine traditions of the Lord—should be rejected.[18]

So what did the first Christians say about Jesus? Answer: the first Christians spread the good news of Jesus, telling the story about Jesus. There would have been a need for such telling of the story from the very beginning, even if some of it would have been well-known in Jerusalem and Galilee.[19] Acts is entirely plausible in its

---

16. Bruce Chilton, A *Galilean Rabbi and His Bible* (London: SPCK, 1984), 84, rightly comments that "a purely literary relationship among the Gospels is problematic. . . . Even if one Gospel is prior to another from a literary point of view, it does not follow it is more historically reliable than its successors. The latter judgment depends on the intent of the writer and the information available to him; Luke, for example, quite evidently thought he could produce a more orderly account than his predecessors."

17. And also to echoes in other non-Pauline Epistles and writings.

18. That is not to encourage parallelomania; it is to encourage a greater awareness of the reality, the priority, and the importance of early oral tradition.

19. Hence the focus in the earliest speeches in Acts on (1) making sense of the recent death of Jesus, especially from the Scriptures, and (2) witnessing to the resurrection.

portrayal of the first disciples as witnessing to Jesus and teaching about him.

Exactly how they did that is impossible to say, but it is likely that a body of what Luke calls "the apostles' teaching" took shape very quickly and became something like an authoritative standard version of events to be "passed on" to converts and those interested in hearing. It is likely that—just as modern evangelists will present a very similar message again and again, tweaked for the particular audience—early evangelists consistently communicated a stable apostolic gospel. And certainly, when the message started to be taken out by people who were not original eyewitnesses, it was necessary to have a memorable account of Jesus to proclaim. Such a tradition or traditions would have been in Aramaic first, but a Greek version would have quickly developed.

These oral traditions would have been similar to our canonical gospels.[20] Admittedly, the evidence for such traditions is varied and not of equal strength. Nevertheless, different pieces of evidence offer a compelling portrait of the prominence of extensive oral traditions in early communication about Jesus.

An objection that has been raised to the idea of a strong oral tradition in the early church is the level of variation among the canonical gospels. Intriguingly this is almost the opposite of the equally hazardous argu-

20. It is striking how even conservative commentators on Paul fail very often to remember and to reflect on the fact that Paul's primary text is not the Old Testament (despite the frequency of his quotations), but the story of Jesus, which he received.

ment, already discussed, that the agreements between the canonical gospels are too great to be explained via oral tradition. Some contend that a stable oral message could not result in the variety attested within Matthew, Mark, Luke, and John. However, this presupposes that the apostolic version (or versions) muted other witnesses. That is unlikely. In the decades after the death of Jesus, there were living eyewitnesses—including most of the apostles—active in the church who carried enormous weight, equal indeed to the emerging shared apostolic tradition.[21] Even if Peter, for example, was a major player in the development of that common tradition, it is entirely unlikely that he just reproduced that material when telling people about Jesus. He and others who had seen the Lord would have reproduced much of it—they had been the main source of the material—but they would not have felt rigidly tied to one particular shared apostolic form, despite its importance. They would have felt entirely free to retell the story, bringing in other perspectives and experiences. It is quite probable that the oral tradition on which the evangelists drew was more extensive—perhaps much more extensive—than any of our written accounts. The evangelists omitted things in the tradition that might have not have suited their purposes or were confusing to their readers. They retained those things that were important.[22] None of our

21. Compare Papias's stated preference for the 'living' voice, even after the writing of the gospels (Eusebius, *Hist. eccl.* 3.39.4). See also Bauckham, *Jesus and the Eyewitnesses*, ch. 20.

22. Much of the work that I have done, notably on the eschatological

writers was a scribe copying out ancient traditions word for word. Each of them was familiar with the emerging standard form of the story about Jesus. Yet, each of them uniquely shaped the traditions.

So Matthew has, arguably, retained some of the teaching of Jesus about the kingdom and "righteousness," while both Mark and Luke have omitted the righteousness sayings, as well as the apparently anti-Gentile sayings of Jesus (such as 10:5; 15:24). Luke, if he spent years in Palestine researching his account of Jesus, reproduced parts of Mark and of the oral tradition but added and omitted material to produce what is very much his own version of the story of Jesus, designed for Theophilus and others like him.[23] Much the same could be said about John—even though John is different from the others and arguably a more personal version that is less tied to the tradition.[24] It is very much the good news "according to" John.[25]

---

discourse, suggests this, and it is not unlikely, given the costliness and constraints of producing written versions. Note the various hints in Mark 4:33 ("with many such parables"), Mark 12:38 ("in his teaching"), and John 21:30. See also Bauckham, *Jesus and the Eyewitnesses*, ch. 21, on oral tradition and gospel divergences.

23. If he was a companion of Paul, then it is quite likely that he knew the version of the tradition taught and used in the Pauline churches (e.g., of the Lord's Supper), although he may also have been one of the people who helped shape that Pauline tradition. It is entirely plausible that he heard and learned other traditions and other versions of stories, in his "investigating" (Luke 1:3). It is this sort of consideration that is at least a partial answer to the comment that the wide divergences between the infancy narratives of Matthew and Luke disprove the idea of a strong oral tradition.

24. See ch. 4 above.

25. It is the individuality of Matthew, Mark, Luke, and John that

The early church refers to all the canonical gospels in that way, not as the "Gospels of Matthew, Mark, etc.," but as the "Gospel *according to* Matthew, *according to* Mark, etc." How far back this nomenclature goes is not certain. Yet, these titles affirm the argument here: Matthew, Mark, Luke, and John are all versions of "the" gospel, a narrative proclaimed by the earliest Christians.[26] They are all, with John being a partial exception, based on the widely known oral tradition—the apostolic gospel passed down and received, but they represent four takes on that gospel. It seems likely that the desirability of putting down "the gospel" in writing became clear, not least as the years passed and the apostles were getting older. So Mark's Gospel quite likely reflects Peter's version, and the others follow. In the early church the canonical gospels were referred to as the "reminiscences" of the apostles.[27] In two senses that might be seen to be a valid judgment. First, the oral tradition was precisely the apostolic teaching in origin. Second, the particular canonical gospels were the versions of that teaching associated with Peter and others.[28]

---

makes redaction criticism a continuingly fruitful exercise, even though it is important to reckon with the oral tradition as a major ingredient in their gospel-writing.

26. See on this Hengel, *The Four Gospels*, 48–56, and Bauckham, *Jesus the Eyewitnesses*, ch. 19. Both scholars doubt that the gospels ever circulated anonymously. The name of the author would have been widely known.

27. Justin, *1 Apol.* 67.3.

28. One of the questions that has been much discussed by scholars is the question of "genre." Richard Burridge, *What Are the Gospels?* 2nd ed. (Grand Rapids: Eerdmans, 2004), argues that the canonical gospels are akin to Graeco-Roman biography. It is quite possible that someone like Luke would have been influenced by that genre of literature. If it is

Some of this discussion of how the earliest tradition evolved is necessarily speculative. But the case for the priority of oral tradition is strong, as is the argument that the early oral tradition was substantial and coherent.[29] The journey from the spoken "good news" of the first Christians to the written gospels of the New Testament was nothing like as tortuous or uncertain as some people suppose. Indeed there was a continuous highway of oral tradition. And what first Christians told people about Jesus was essentially the story in the written gospels as now preserved.

For too long, the study of the gospels (and other parts of the New Testament) has operated without a full appreciation of the substantial oral tradition about Jesus. If the arguments of this book—and of other scholars pressing the case for the priority of oral tradition—are correct and are taken seriously, then new perspectives on the biblical texts and new understandings of the history of earliest Christianity are bound to follow.

---

right to suppose that the earliest accounts of Jesus's life are essentially the proclamation of the first believers turned into book form, then perhaps they should be explained as that, and not primarily in literary categories.

29. E. P. Sanders famously proposed categories of plausibility for his arguments: 1. Certain or virtually certain; 2. Highly probable; 3. Probable; 4. Possible; 5. Conceivable; 6. Incredible; see his *Jesus and Judaism* (London: SCM, 1985), 326. I would categorize my most ambitious claims (about an oral tradition resembling the written gospels) as probable or possible, whereas I rate my main but less ambitious arguments (about the existence of a very early strong and coherent oral tradition, about its priority, and about its importance for understanding the gospels and the New Testament) near the top of the probability scale. From the very beginning of the church's life, the story of Jesus was the key ingredient in what the first Christians said and believed.

Bibliography

Alexander, Loveday. *The Preface to Luke's Gospel: Literary Convention and Social Context in Luke 1:1–4 and Acts 1:1.* Cambridge: Cambridge University Press, 2005.

Allison, Dale C. *Constructing Jesus: Memory, Imagination, and History.* Grand Rapids: Baker, 2010.

Aslan, Reza. *Zealot: The Life and Times of Jesus of Nazareth.* London: Westbourne, 2013.

Bailey, Kenneth E. "Informal Controlled Oral Tradition and the Synoptic Gospels." *Themelios* 20 (1995): 4–11.

———. "Middle Eastern Oral Tradition and the Synoptic Gospels." *ExpT* 106 (1995): 363–67.

Bammel, Ernst. "Judenverfolgung und Naherwartung. Zur Eschatologie des ersten Thessaloicherbriefs." *ZTK* 56 (1959): 294–315.

Bauckham, Richard. "Eyewitnesses and Critical History: A Response to Jens Schröter and Craig Evans." *JSNT* 31 (2008): 221–35.

———. "In Response to My Respondents: Jesus and the Eyewitnesses in Review." *Journal for the Study of the Historical Jesus* 6 (2008): 225–53.

————. *Jesus and the Eyewitnesses: The Gospels as Eyewitness Testimony*. 2nd ed. Grand Rapids: Eerdmans, 2017.

————. *The Testimony of the Beloved Disciple: Narrative, History, and Theology in the Gospel of John*. Grand Rapids: Baker, 2007.

Baum, Armin. *Der mündliche Faktor und seine Bedeutung für die synoptische Frage*. Tübingen: Francke, 2008.

Beasley-Murray, G. R. *A Commentary on Mark 13*. London: Macmillan, 1957.

Bird, Michael F. *The Gospel of the Lord: How the Early Church Wrote the Story of Jesus*. Grand Rapids: Eerdmans, 2014.

Bowman, James. *The Gospel of Mark: The New Christian Jewish Passover Haggadah*. Leiden: Brill, 1965.

Bultmann, Rudolf. *The History of the Synoptic Tradition*. Translated by John Marsh. Oxford: Blackwell, 1963.

Burridge, Richard. *What Are the Gospels? A Comparison with Graeco-Roman Biography*. 2nd ed. Grand Rapids: Eerdmans, 2004.

Byrskog, Samuel. "The Eyewitnesses as Interpreters of the Past: Reflections on Richard Bauckham's Jesus and the Eyewitnesses." *Journal for the Study of the Historical Jesus* 6.2 (2008): 157–68.

————. *Jesus the Only Teacher: Didactic Authority and Transmission in Ancient Israel, Ancient Judaism and the Matthean Community*. Coniectanea Biblica New Testament Series 24. Stockholm: Almqvist & Wiksell International, 1994.

————. *Story as History—History as Story: The Gospel Tradition in the Context of Ancient Oral History*. WUNT 123. Tübingen: Mohr Siebeck, 2000.

Casey, Maurice. *Jesus of Nazareth: An Independent Historian's Account of His Life and Teaching*. London: Black, 2002.

Catchpole, David. "On Proving Too Much: Critical Hesitations about Richard Bauckham's Jesus and the Eyewitnesses." *Journal for the Study of the Historical Jesus* 6 (2008): 169–81.

Chilton, Bruce. *A Galilean Rabbi and His Bible*. London: SPCK, 1984.

Ciampa, Roy E., and Brian S. Rosner. *The First Letter to the Corinthians*. Nottingham: Apollos, 2010.

Cranfield, C. E. B. "Some Reflections on the Subject of the Virgin Birth." *SJT* 41 (1988): 177–98.

Crossan, John Dominic. *The Birth of Christianity: Discovering What Happened in the Years Immediately after the Execution of Jesus*. Edinburgh: T&T Clark, 1999.

Davies, W. D., and Dale C. Allison. *The Gospel according to Saint Matthew*. Vol. 3. Edinburgh: T&T Clark, 1997.

Derico, Travis. *Oral Tradition and the Synoptic Verbal Agreement: Evaluating the Empirical Evidence for Literary Dependence*. Eugene, OR: Pickwick, 2016.

Dodd, C. H. *The Apostolic Preaching and Its Developments*. London: Hodder, 1936.

Dungan, David L. *The Sayings of Jesus in the Churches of Paul*. Oxford: Blackwell, 1971.

Dunn, James D. G. "Altering the Default Setting: Re-envisaging the Early Transmission of the Jesus Tradition." *NTS* 49 (2003): 139–75.

———. *Jesus, Paul, and the Law*. Westminster: John Knox, 1990.

———. *Jesus Remembered*. Vol. 1 of *Christianity in the Making*. Grand Rapids: Eerdmans, 2003.

———. *The Oral Gospel Tradition*. Grand Rapids: Eerdmans, 2013.

———. "Social Memory and the Oral Jesus Tradition." Pages 179–94 in *Memory in the Bible and Antiquity*. Edited by Loren T. Stuckenbruck, Stephen C. Barton, and Benjamin G. Wold. WUNT 212. Tübingen: Mohr Siebeck, 2007.

Ellis, E. Earle. *Christ and the Future in New Testament History*. NovTSup 97. Leiden: Brill, 2001.

Evans, Craig A. "The Implications of Eyewitness Tradition." *JSNT* 31 (2008): 211–19.

Eve, Eric. *Behind the Gospels: Understanding the Oral Tradition*. London: SPCK, 2013.

Farmer, William R. *The Synoptic Problem: A Critical Analysis.* Macon: Mercer University Press, 1976.

Fjärstedt, Biörn. *Synoptic Tradition in 1 Corinthians: Themes and Clusters of Theme Words in 1 Corinthians 1–4 and 9.* Thesis, Uppsala, 1974.

Funk, Robert W., and Roy W. Hoover, eds. *The Five Gospels.* San Francisco: HarperSanFrancisco, 1997.

Garrow, Alan. "The Eschatological Tradition behind 1 Thessalonians: Didache 16." *JSNT* 32 (2009): 191–215.

———. *The Gospel of Matthew's Dependence on the Didache.* JSNTSup 254. London: T&T Clark, 2004.

———. "Streeter's 'Other' Synoptic Solution: The Matthew Conflator Hypothesis." *NTS* 62 (2016): 207–26.

Gerhardsson, Birger. *Memory and Manuscript: Oral Tradition and Written Transmission in Rabbinic Judaism and Early Christianity.* 3rd ed. Grand Rapids: Eerdmans, 1998.

———. *The Reliability of the Gospel Tradition.* Peabody, MA: Hendrickson, 2001.

———. "The Secret of the Transmission of the Unwritten Jesus Tradition." *NTS* 51 (2005): 1–18.

Goodacre, Mark S. *The Synoptic Problem: A Way through the Maze.* London: Sheffield Academic, 1996.

Gundry, Robert H. *Peter: False Disciple and Apostate according to Saint Matthew.* Grand Rapids: Eerdmans, 2015.

Hagner, Donald A. *The New Testament: A Historical and Theological Introduction.* Grand Rapids: Baker, 2012.

———. "The Sayings of Jesus in the Apostolic Fathers and Justin Martyr." Pages 233–68 in *The Jesus Tradition outside the Gospels.* Edited by David Wenham. Vol. 5 of *Gospel Perspectives.* Sheffield: JSOT, 1985.

Häusser, Detlef. *Christusbekenntnis und Jesusüberlieferung bei Paulus.* WUNT 2.210. Tübingen: Mohr Siebeck, 2006.

Hays, Richard B. *The Faith of Jesus Christ: An Investigation of the Narrative Substructure of Galatians 3:1–4:11.* Chico: Scholars, 1983.

Hemer, Colin. *The Book of Acts in the Context of Hellenistic History.* Winona Lake: Eisenbrauns, 1989.

Hengel, Martin. *The Four Gospels and the One Gospel of Jesus Christ.* London: SCM, 2000.

Hultren, Stephen. *Narrative Elements in the Double Tradition: A Study of Their Place within the Framework of the Gospel Narrative.* Berlin: Walter de Gruyter, 2002.

Jacobi, Christine. *Jesusüberlieferung bei Paulus? Analogien zwischen den echten Paulusbriefen und den synoptischen Evangelien.* Berlin: Walter de Gruyter, 2015.

Jeremias, Joachim. *New Testament Theology.* London: SCM, 1971.

Kang, Boyoung. *Heralds and Community: An Enquiry into Paul's Conception of Mission and Its Indebtedness to the Jesus-Tradition.* Carlisle: Langham, 2016.

Keener, Craig S. *Acts. An Exegetical Commentary.* 4 vols. Grand Rapids: Baker, 2012–2015.

Keith, Chris. "Memory and Authenticity. Jesus Tradition and What Really Happened." *ZNW* 102 (2011): 155–77.

Kelber, Werner H. *The Oral and the Written Gospel: The Hermeneutics of Speaking and Writing in the Synoptic Tradition, Mark, Paul, and Q.* Bloomington: Indiana University Press, 1997.

Lambrecht, Jan. *Die Redaktion der Markus-Apokalypse.* Rome: Pontifical Institute, 1967.

Lapide, Pinchas. *The Resurrection of Jesus: A Jewish Perspective.* London: SPCK, 1984.

Lee, Yongbom. *Paul. Scribe of Old and New: Intertextual Insights for the Jesus-Paul Debate.* Edinburgh: T&T Clark, 2015.

———. *The Son of Man As the Last Adam.* Eugene, OR: Pickwick, 2012.

Lierman, John, ed. *Challenging Perspectives on the Gospel of John.* WUNT 2.219. Tübingen: Mohr Siebeck, 2006.

Lincoln, Andrew. *Born of a Virgin? Reconceiving Jesus in the Bible, Tradition and Theology.* Grand Rapids: Eerdmans, 2013.

Luz, Ulrich. "The Use of Jesus-Traditions in the Pauline and Post-

Pauline Letters." Pages 75–91 in *Exegetische Aufsätze*. WUNT 357. Tübingen: Mohr Siebeck, 2016.

Macdonald, Margaret Y. "Women Holy in Body and Spirit in the Social Setting of 1 Corinthians 7." *NTS* 36 (1990): 161–81.

Marcus, Joel. *Mark 1–8: A New Translation*. AB 27. New York: Doubleday, 1999.

Marshall, I. Howard. "A New Consensus on Oral Tradition? A Review of Richard Bauckham's Jesus and the Eyewitnesses." *Journal for the Study of the Historical Jesus* 6 (2008): 182–93.

McIver, Robert K. *Memory, Jesus, and the Synoptic Gospels*. Atlanta: Society of Biblical Literature, 2011.

Meier, John P. *The Roots of the Problem and the Person*. Vol. 1 of *A Marginal Jew: Rethinking the Historical Jesus*. New York: Doubleday, 1991.

Ninan, Idicheria. *Jesus as the Son of God: An Examination of the Background and Meaning of "Son of God" in Paul's Christology with Particular Reference to Romans 8*. PhD diss., Coventry University, 1994.

Pahl, Michael W. *Discerning the "Word of the Lord": The "Word of the Lord" in 1 Thessalonians 4:15*. London: T&T Clark, 2009.

Patterson, Stephen J. "Can You Trust a Gospel? A Review of Richard Bauckham's Jesus and the Eyewitnesses." *Journal for the Study of the Historical Jesus* 6 (2008): 194–210.

Pervo, Richard I. *Acts: A Commentary*. Hermeneia. Philadelphia: Fortress, 2009.

Porter, Stanley. *When Paul Met Jesus: How An Idea Got Lost in History*. Cambridge: Cambridge University Press, 2016.

Rapske, Brian M. "Acts, Travel and Shipwreck." Pages 1–47 in *The Book of Acts in Its Graeco-Roman Setting*. Edited by David W. J. Gill and Conrad Gempf. Vol. 2 of *The Book of Acts in Its First Century Setting*. Grand Rapids: Eerdmans, 1994.

Reicke, Bo. *The Roots of the Synoptic Gospels*. Philadelphia: Fortress, 1986.

Riesenfeld, Harald. *The Gospel Tradition and Its Beginnings: A Study in the Limits of "Formgeschichte".* London: Mowbray, 1957.

Riesner, Rainer. *Jesus als Lehrer: Eine Untersuchung zum Ursprung der Evangelien-Überlieferung.* WUNT 2.7. Tübingen: Mohr Siebeck, 1981.

———. "Jesus as Preacher and Teacher." Pages 185–210 in *Jesus and the Oral Gospel Tradition.* Edited by Henry Wansbrough. JSNTSup 64. Sheffield: JSOT, 1991.

———. "The Orality and Memory Hypothesis." Pages 89–111, 151–63 in *The Synoptic Problem: Four Views.* Edited by Stanley E. Porter and Bryan R. Dyer. Grand Rapids: Baker, 2016.

———. *Paul's Early Period: Chronology, Mission Strategy, Theology.* Grand Rapids: Eerdmans, 1998.

———. "Paulus und die Jesus-Überlieferung." Pages 347–65 in *Evangelium Schriftauslegung Kirche. Festschrift für Peter Stuhlmacher zum 65. Geburtstag.* Edited by Jostein Ådna, Scott J. Hafemann, and Otfried Hofius. Göttingen: Vandenhoeck & Ruprecht, 1997.

Rist, John M. *On the Independence of Matthew and Mark.* Cambridge: Cambridge University Press, 2005.

Sanders, E. P. *Jesus and Judaism.* London: SCM, 1985.

Schlueter, Carol J. *Filling up the Measure: Polemical Hyperbole in 1 Thessalonians 2:14–16.* Sheffield: JSOT, 1994.

Schoberg, Gerry. *Perspectives of Jesus in the Writings of Paul: A Historical Examination of Shared Core Commitments with a View to Determining the Extent of Paul's Dependence on Jesus.* Cambridge: James Clarke, 2014.

Schröter, Jens. *From Jesus to the New Testament. Early Christian Theology and the Jesus Traditions.* Translated by Wayne Coppins. Tübingen: Mohr Siebeck; Waco: Baylor University Press, 2013.

———. "The Gospels as Eyewitness Testimony? A Critical Examination of Richard Bauckham's Jesus and the Eyewitnesses." *JSNT* 31 (2008): 195–209.

————. "Jesus and the Canon: The Early Jesus Traditions in the Context of the Origins of the New Testament Canon." Pages 104–22 in *Performing the Gospel: Orality, Memory and Mark*. Edited by Richard A. Horsley, Jonathan A. Draper, and John Miles Foley. Minneapolis: Fortress, 2006.

Stanton, Graham N. *The Gospels and Jesus*. Oxford: Oxford University Press, 1989.

————. *Jesus of Nazareth in New Testament Proclaiming*. Cambridge: Cambridge University Press, 1974.

Stenschke, Christoph W. "The Jewish Savior for Israel in the Missionary Speeches of Acts." In *The Earliest Perceptions of Jesus in Context: Essays in Honour of John Nolland*. Edited by A. W. White, David Wenham, and Craig A. Evans. London: T&T Clark, forthcoming.

Stettler, Hanna. *Heiligung bei Paulus: Ein Beitrag aus biblisch-theologischer Sicht*. WUNT 2.368. Tübingen: Mohr Siebeck, 2014.

Streeter, B. H. *The Four Gospels*. London: Macmillan, 1930.

Tan, Kim Huat. *Mark: A New Covenant Commentary*. Cambridge: Lutterworth, 2016.

Thiselton, Anthony C. *The First Epistle to the Corinthians: A Commentary on the Greek Text*. NIGTC. Grand Rapids: Eerdmans, 2000.

Thompson, Michael B. *Clothed with Christ: The Example and Teaching of Jesus in Romans 12:1–15:13*. Sheffield: JSOT, 1991.

Thornton, Claus-Jürgen. *Der Zeuge des Zeugen Lukas als Historiker der Paulusreisen*. WUNT 56. Tübingen: Mohr Siebeck, 1991.

Wansbrough, Henry, ed. *Jesus and the Oral Gospel Tradition*. Sheffield: JSOT, 1991.

Watson, Francis. "How Did Mark Survive?" Pages 1–17 in *Matthew and Mark across Perspectives: Essays in Honour of Stephen C. Barton and William R. Telford*. Edited by Kristian A. Bendoraitis and Nijay K. Gupta. London: T&T Clark, 2016.

Weeden, Theodore J. "Polemics as a Case for Dissent: A Response to Richard Bauckham's Jesus and the Eyewitnesses." *Journal for the Study of the Historical Jesus* 6 (2008): 211–24.

Wenham, David. "Acts and the Pauline Corpus II. The Evidence of Parallels." Pages 215–58 in *Ancient Literary Setting*. Edited by Bruce W. Winter and Andrew D. Clarke. Vol. 1 of *The Book of Acts in Its First Century Setting*. Grand Rapids: Eerdmans, 1993.

———. "Critical Blindness, Wise Virgins, and the Law of Christ: Three Surprising Examples of Jesus Tradition in Paul." Pages 183–203 in *The Message of Jesus: John Dominic Crossan and Ben Witherington III in Dialogue*. Edited by Robert B. Stewart. Augsburg: Fortress, 2013.

———. "Matthean Priority: You Must Be Joking!" In *Treasures New and Old: Essays in Honor of Donald A. Hagner*. Edited by Craig A. Evans, Cliff B. Kvidahl, and Matthew D. Montonini. Wilmore, KY: GlossaHouse, 2017.

———. *Paul and Jesus: The True Story*. London: SPCK, 2002.

———. *Paul: Follower of Jesus or Founder of Christianity?* Grand Rapids: Eerdmans, 1995.

———. "Paul's Use of the Jesus Tradition: Three Samples." Pages 7–15 in *The Jesus Tradition Outside the Gospels*. Edited by David Wenham. Vol. 5 of *Gospel Perspectives*. Sheffield: JSOT, 1985.

———. *The Rediscovery of Jesus' Eschatological Discourse*. Sheffield: JSOT, 1984.

———. "The Rock on Which to Build: Some Mainly Pauline Observations about the Sermon on the Mount." Pages 186–206 in *Built Upon the Rock: Studies in the Gospel of Matthew*. Edited by Daniel M. Gurtner and John Nolland. Grand Rapids: Eerdmans, 2007.

Wenham, John. *Redating Matthew, Mark and Luke*. London: Hodder, 1991.

Westcott, B. F. *Introduction to the Study of the Gospels*. London: Macmillan, 1895.

Wright, N. T. *Jesus and the Victory of God*. Vol. 2 of *Christian Origins and the Question of God*. Minneapolis: Fortress, 1996.

Yeung, Maureen W. *Faith in Jesus and Paul: A Comparison with Special Reference to "Faith That Can Remove Mountains" and "Your Faith Has Healed/Saved You"*. WUNT 2.147. Tübingen: Mohr Siebeck, 2002.

Author Index

Alexander, Loveday, 21n14
Allison, Dale C., 42n11, 81n12
Aslan, Reza, 3n5

Bailey, Kenneth E., ix–xi, xiii, xiv, 6n11
Bammel, Ernst, 23n17
Bauckham, Richard, 10n13, 27–28, 32n6, 67n5, 105n21, 106n22, 107n26
Baum, Armin, 10n13, 14n2, 100n11, 101n13
Beasley-Murray, G. R., 82n15
Bird, Michael F., 6n11, 10n13, 15n6, 29n3, 66n2, 72n11, 99n8
Bowman, James, 5n9
Bultmann, Rudolf, xn8, 66n3
Burridge, Richard, 107n28
Byrskog, Samuel, xii, xvi, 10n13, 28n2

Casey, Maurice, 3n5
Catchpole, David, 28n2
Chilton, Bruce, 103n16
Ciampa, Roy E., 77n6
Cranfield, C. E. B., 89n6
Crossan, John Dominic, 10n13

Derico, Travis, 6n11, 10n13, 100n11
Dodd, C. H., 97n2
Dungan, David L., 76n5
Dunn, James D. G., ix, x, 10, 11n14, 53n31, 56, 86n21, 98n7, 99n8

Ellis, E. Earle, 101n14
Evans, Craig A., 28n2
Eve, Eric, 10n13

Farmer, William R., 12n16
Fjärstedt, Biörn, 47n17
Funk, Robert W., viii

Garrow, Alan, 72n11, 83n16
Gerhardsson, Birger, viii, x–xvi, 10n13, 14
Goodacre, Mark S., 66n2, 72–73n11
Gundry, Robert H., 86n20

Hagner, Donald A., 10n13, 11n15
Häusser, Detlef, 59n40
Hays, Richard B., 56n33, 92n8
Hemer, Colin, 22n15, 24n18
Hengel, Martin, 28n2, 107n26
Hoover, Roy W., viii
Hultgren, Stephen, 94n10

Jacobi, Christine, 59n40
Jeremias, Joachim, 71n8

Kang, Boyoung, 47n17
Keener, Craig S., 22n15
Keith, Chris, 10n14
Kelber, Werner H., ix, 10n13, 69n7

Lambrecht, Jan, 82n15
Lapide, Pinchas, 3n5
Lee, Yongbom, 56n33, 59n39
Lierman, John, 32n6
Lincoln, Andrew, 89–90n6
Luz, Ulrich, 37, 43n13, 45n15, 52n27,
    56–59, 87n2, 88, 89n3, 97n2

Macdonald, Margaret Y., 45n15
Marcus, Joel, 52n28
Marshall, I. Howard, 28n2
McIver, Robert K., 10n13
Meier, John P., 35n8

Ninan, Idicheria, 92n8

Pahl, Michael W., 50n22
Patterson, Stephen J., 28n2
Pervo, Richard I., 21n12
Porter, Stanley, 61n41

Rapske, Brian M., 25n20
Reicke, Bo, 10n20, 101n13
Riesenfeld, Harald, 9–10n13
Riesner, Rainer, xiii–iv, 10n13, 14n4,
    22n15, 57n35, 100n11, 101n14

Rist, John M., 101n13
Rosner, Brian S., 77n6

Sanders, E. P., 108n29
Schlueter, Carol J., 23–24n17
Schoberg, Gerry, 58n36
Schröter, Jens, 28n2, 40n10, 45n14,
    50–51n24, 59n40
Stanton, Graham N., 8–9, 95–96,
    99n8
Stenschke, Christoph W., 19n9,
    20n11
Stettler, Hanna, 53n30
Streeter, B. H., 66n2

Tan, Kim Huat, 28n2
Thiselton, Anthony C., 36n2
Thompson, Michael B., 47–48n19,
    51n25
Thornton, Claus-Jürgen, 24n19

Watson, Francis, 102n14
Weeden, Theodore J., 28n2
Wenham, David, ix, 22n15, 23n17,
    50n23, 53n30, 59n40, 72n10,
    76n4, 77n5, 82n14, 84n18, 86n20,
    88n2
Wenham, John, 5n9
Westcott, B. F., 65
Wright, N. T., x

Yeung, Maureen W., 58n36

Subject Index

Abba, 41–43
Acts, 15–26
Apocryphal gospels, 35
Apostles/disciples, 14–16, 29–31, 46–47, 60–63, 104

Creeds, 7–8, 91–93

Dating of the New Testament, 2, 4–5, 36, 46n16
Divorce, 45–46

Eschatological teaching, 47–50, 77–85
Ethical teaching, 45–46, 51–55

Form criticism, 5–6, 66–69

Gospel/good news, 2–8, 15–20, 28–30, 34–44, 60–64, 90–95, 103–4

Jesus: xi–xiv, 1–6, 13–15, 36–55, 58–59, 87–94; birth, 89; death, 2, 41–43; Last Supper, 39–41; ministry, 44–46; resurrection, 38–39; teacher, xi–xiii, 13–14, 44–60, 74–86
Jesus Seminar, viii–ix
Jews and Gentiles, 75–77
John, 31–34, 55

Law of Christ, 54–56
Luke, 19–20, 24–26

Mark, 13, 27–30, 52–53, 80–82
Matthew, 30–31, 49–50, 75–76, 85–86.
Memory, xiii–xvi, 9n13, 14, 70–71, 99–100.

Oral tradition, vii–xiv, 9–12, 36–41, 65, 68–73, 81–89, 96–101, 107–8

Parables, 47–50, 77–83
Paul, 36–64, 75–76, 83–86, 88–94

Q, 5, 65–73, 74–86, 88, 98–101

Synoptic problem, 65–73, 74–86, 98–102

Witness, 16, 33–34

Biblical References Index

Isaiah

52:7	29n3

Matthew

2:1–15	75n3
3:12	70
5:10	59n38
5:16	97
5:17	52
5:17–20	53n31
5:20	59
5:20–48	52
5:43–45	51
7:24–27	30
8:23–27	67
9:37–10:16	74
10	15
10:5	106
10:5–6	75–77
10:8	46n16, 76n4
10:11	46, 74
12:28	70
13:11	71
13:31–33	72
13:51	31n4
13:52	14n3
14:33	31n4
14:44	31n4

15:17–20	53n31
15:24	77, 106
16:15–17	85n20
16:16	86n20
16:16–20	62n42, 86n20
16:17–20	31n5
16:23	31n5
18:12–14	67
18:17	77n6
20:25–26	55
22:34–40	51
23:8	xii
23:8–11	55
23:10	xii
23:11	54
24–25	74
24:29–31	49, 50n23
24:30–31	83–84
24:42	79
24:43	47, 77
24:45–51	78
25:1–13	49–50, 78
25:14–30	78–79
26:68	71
28:16–20	30, 31, 75–76
28:19	93

Mark

1:1	28–29
1:14	2n2, 29n3
1:17	29
1:22	xi, 13
1:27	xi
2:14	29
3:14	30
3:22–27	70
4	68–69
4:1–2	13
4:10	31n4
4:10–11	88n2
4:11	71
4:14	2n2
4:30–32	72, 88n2
4:33	87n1, 106n22
4:35–41	67
6	15
6:7–13	15, 74
6:12	2n2
6:51–52	31n4
7:3–4	52n29
7:16–19	52
7:27	77n6
7:29	xi
8:27–30	xii
8:29	85–86n20

8:34	29–30	11:20	70	2:32	16
9:35	54	12:35	50n13, 78n9,	2:42	16
10:9–12	45–46		79, 83n16	3:15	16
10:17	14n3	12:35–38	79–81	5:35–37	21n13
10:42–43	55	12:35–48	79	6:2–4	16
10:43–45	46n16,	12:39	47, 77	6:4	20
	54–55	12:41	80	6:7	2n2
12:28	106n22	12:41–46	78	8:5	2n2
12:28–34	51	13:18–19	88n1	9	24n20
12:38	87n1, 106n22	13:18–21	72	9:2–28	22n16
12:38–40	76–77n5	13:25	79–90n11	10:34–43	97
13:10	29n3, 30	15:3–7	67	10:36–43	17–19
13:24–27	49	19:12–27	78–79	10:39	16
13:26–27	83–84	21	84	11:22–26	22n16
13:32	81n12	21:25–28	49	11:27–29	22n16
13:33–37	76–77n5,	21:27	83–84	12:12	27n1
	80–82	21:34–36	83	13:7	24
14:36	42	22:7–23	40n9	13:10	30
14:45	14n3	22:24–27	54	13:16–41	17
14:51–52	28n2	22:25–26	55	14	17
14:65	71	22:64	71	15	22n16
15:22	28n2	24:34	40n9	15:37–38	93n9
		24:46–49	93	15:39	27n1
				16:10	24
Luke		**John**		16:22	24
1–2	93	3–4	31n6	17:6	24
1:1–4	20, 21	5:2	31n6	18	2n4, 23n17
1:3	106n23	5:30–47	33	18:2	23–24
1:34	89	13:4–17	54	18:12	24
1:68	89	13:34	31–32n6	19:31	24
2:1–3	21n13	13:34–35	55	20:35	16–17n8
2:22–27	89	15:26–27	33	22–26	24n20
3:1–3	21	20:26–28	32	27	25n20
3:17	70	20:29	32–33	28:7	24
4:16–30	68	20:30–31	32	28:30–31	19
4:32	xi	21:24	32–34		
6:27–28	51	21:30	106	**Romans**	
8:10	71			1:1–4	97
9–10	47	**Acts**		1:1–5	61, 91–93
9:1–9	74	1	15–16, 20n11, 30	1:3	89
9:3–5	15	1:21–22	20	1:3–4	63
9:20	86n20	1:22	2n2	1:16	76
10:1–37	74	2:14–36	17	8:15	42n12
10:7	46, 74				

10:15–18	2n2
12–15	51n25
12–13	51
12:14–19	51
13:8–10	51
14:14	52
14:17	59
15:8	76, 77

1 Corinthians

4:1–4	78n8, 79
4:12	51n26
4:20	59
5:3–5	77n6
6:9	59
6:12–13	53
7:8	45n14
7:10–11	7, 45–46
9	46–47, 63
9:1	60, 61
9:8	76n4
9:14	46–47, 50–51n24, 63
9:18	46n16
9:19	46n16, 55
11	75
11:23	36
11:23–26	7, 39–41, 51n24
11:23b-25	51n24
12	78n10
13	51
15	61–63, 75
15:1	92
15:1–2	36
15:1–3	38–41
15:1–4	3–4, 7
15:1–11	63
15:5	40n9
15:8	61
15:9	60

2 Corinthians

5:16	37n4
8:7–9	55n32
8:9	89
10:1	89
11:7	76n4

Galatians

1–2	60, 85n20
1	62
1:12	37n4, 62, 86n20
1:13–24	39n8
1:15–17	86n20
1:16	61, 86n20
2:1–10	23n16, 62
2:7–8	62, 85n20
2:7–9	76
2:8	62n42
3:1	41, 62n42
3:13	92n8
4:4	41, 89
4:4–5	90n6, 92n8
4:6	41–42, 62n42
4:21–31	90n6
4:33–34	89–90
5:13	55, 62n42
6:2	54, 55
6:17	41

Ephesians

4:11	93n9

Philippians

2	89
2:5–11	7, 55, 92
2:7	89

Colossians

4:10	27n1

1 Thessalonians

1:6	89
1:9–10	48

2:15	43n13
2:17	23n17
4–5	84
4	78, 83
4:13–18	49–50
4:15	48n20
4:15–19	50n24
5:2	47–48, 77
5:2–4	84

2 Thessalonians

2	84n18
3:8–9	76n4

1 Timothy

5:18	46n16
6:13	43n13

Philemon

24	27n1

Hebrews

5:7	42n11
13:12	42n11

1 Peter

2:12	97n2
3:14	59n38, 97n2
5:13	27n1

2 Peter

3:10	48n20

1 John

3–5	58

Revelation

3:3	48n20
16:15	48n20